THE EVERYTHING KIDS' Baseball BOOK

5TH EDITION

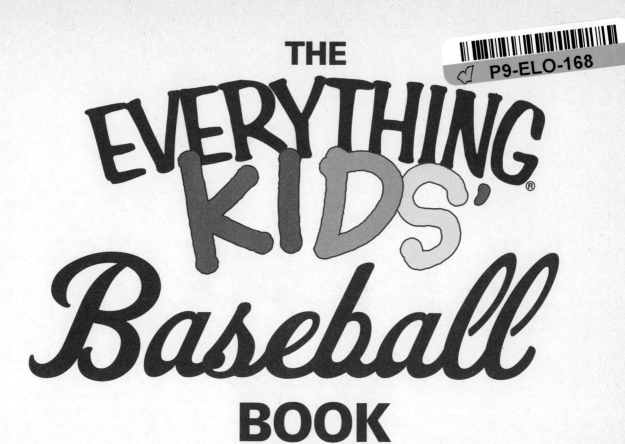

The all-time greats, legendary
teams, today's superstars—
and tips on playing like a pro

Greg Jacobs

Reporter/Statistician, STATS, LLC

adamsmedia
avon, massachusetts

DIRECTOR OF INNOVATION Paula Munier
EDITORIAL DIRECTOR Laura M. Daly
EXECUTIVE EDITOR, SERIES BOOKS Brielle K. Matson
ASSOCIATE COPY CHIEF Sheila Zwiebel
ACQUISITIONS EDITOR Kerry Smith
DEVELOPMENT EDITOR Katie McDonough
PRODUCTION EDITOR Casey Ebert

An Everything® Series Book.
Everything® and everything.com® are registered trademarks of F+W Publications, Inc.

Published by Adams Media, an F+W Publications Company
57 Littlefield Street, Avon, MA 02322. U.S.A.
www.adamsmedia.com

ISBN 10: 1-59869-487-1
ISBN 13: 978-1-59869-487-1

Printed in the United States of America

J I H G F E D C B

This publication is designed to provide accurate and authoritative information with regard to the subject matter covered. It is sold with the understanding that the publisher is not engaged in rendering legal, accounting, or other professional advice. If legal advice or other expert assistance is required, the services of a competent professional person should be sought.
—From a *Declaration of Principles* jointly adopted by a Committee of the American Bar Association and a Committee of Publishers and Associations

Many of the designations used by manufacturers and sellers to distinguish their products are claimed as trademarks. When those designations appear in this book and Adams Media was aware of a trademark claim, the designations have been printed with initial capital letters.

Cover illustrations by Dana Regan.
Interior illustrations by Kurt Dolber.
Puzzles by Beth Blair.
Kids' Logo Design by Dutton and Sherman.

This book is available at quantity discounts for bulk purchases. For information, call 1-800-289-0963.

See the entire Everything® series at *www.everything.com*.

Contents

To Milo Cebu, who wants
to be a Cardinals fan.
(We'll see.)

Introduction

I have loved baseball all my life. Some of my earliest memories are of rooting for the Los Angeles Dodgers against the New York Yankees in the 1977 World Series. I can still remember that great Dodger infield of Steve Garvey at first base, Davey Lopes at second base, Bill Russell at shortstop, and "The Penguin" Ron Cey at third base.

Of this set of my then-favorite players, none made the Hall of Fame. None was the best ever at his position. In fact, I used to get into shouting matches about whether any of these folks was even the best player in 1977.

But even if these players weren't special to anyone else, they were special to me, because I rooted for them when I was a kid. Now, with an extra thirty years or so of perspective, I don't get upset when someone makes fun of Steve Garvey. Instead, I get upset when people don't recognize Johnny Bench as the greatest catcher in history.

The point is, I *care* about baseball. Other adults I know also take the game far more seriously than grown folks probably should. We watch major-league games; we talk about the games; we complain about the players; we stay up past 1:00 in the morning to see the Red Sox beat the Yankees (or vice versa). Why? Because we fell in love with the game when we were your age.

Since your parents were young, major-league baseball has evolved into new stadiums, with new league rules, new teams, and certainly different players. But the links to the past are always present. Maybe your mom's favorite player from when she was a girl is now managing somewhere. Perhaps you could go to a game at Wrigley Field in Chicago, where the Cubs have played since 1914—maybe your great-great-grandfather once attended a game there! Or you could listen to a Dodgers radio broadcast to hear broadcaster Vin Scully, who has been the voice of the Dodgers for fifty years.

The *Everything® KIDS' Baseball Book, 5th Edition* can be your guide to baseball past and baseball present. It's certainly fun to read straight through; but it can also be a useful reference. Are your grandparents always talking about the 1976 World Series? Read about what they saw in this book. Is your dad always staring at the box scores in the newspaper? Use this book to find out what those columns of numbers mean. Do you want to become a better player? This book gives you some ideas for developing your playing skills. Having trouble understanding your brother's fantasy baseball team? This book explains fantasy baseball, so you might be able to give *him* pointers.

There's undoubtedly more to baseball than merely what is contained in this book. Appendix B, or your parents or a librarian, can suggest where to go to find more detail than what is included here. My simple hope is that by reading this book you can start to fall in love with baseball, just like I did years ago.

WORDS to KNOW

inning: A turn at bat for each team is called an inning. A professional or college baseball game lasts for nine innings. High school and little league games are usually shorter—five, six, or seven innings.

Baseball is a great game, and one that is played and enjoyed by tens of millions of people. Many of those who appreciate the game grew up playing and watching baseball. Few get good enough to be a major leaguer, but everyone can learn how to play, and everyone can, with practice, become a better player. This chapter covers the fundamentals of baseball: the rules, the necessary skills, the positions of the players, and some ways to play baseball even if you don't have two teams of nine players available.

Rules of the Game

Baseball, at its heart, is a very simple game. A batter hits the ball, then tries to make it to first base (or farther!) without getting called out. Someone who gets all the way around the bases scores a run; whichever team scores the most runs during the game wins.

Teams take turns at bat. A team keeps batting until they make three outs; then they pitch to the other team until *they* make three outs. After each team has had nine turns, the game is over.

Here are the most common ways for the batter to make an out:

- **Strikeout:** A batter gets a strike if he swings and misses, or if he doesn't swing at a good pitch. Three strikes and the batter is out.
- **Flyout:** If a fielder catches a batted ball before it hits the ground, the batter is out.
- **Groundout:** If a fielder throws the ball to first base before the batter gets there, the batter is out.
- **A base runner can be tagged out, too:** If a runner is not touching a base and is tagged with the ball, the runner is out.

Playing the Game

There's much, much more to the rules of baseball; but you learn as you play and as you watch. Even professional players are still learning about the game. That's part of what makes baseball such a wonderful sport!

Developing Your Baseball Skills

How can you develop your baseball skills? The answer is simple: play. Play a lot. Play with your friends; play in a league or two; play in the backyard with your family. The more you play, the more you'll learn about the game. You'll develop baseball instincts—you'll know what to do on the bases or in the field without even thinking about it. Your skills will get better and better, often before you even notice how good you've gotten. And whether or not you become a great player, you will likely develop a deep appreciation for the game of baseball that you can share with your friends and family. Many adults' most profound memories are of playing and watching baseball when they were kids your age.

For professional baseball you need two teams of nine players, each with uniforms and gloves, several brand-new baseballs, and four umpires . . . but all you *really* need to play a game is a few friends, an old tennis ball, and a stick for a bat. Check out the "fun and games" sections for ideas of how to play baseball anywhere, anytime.

Hitting

To become a good hitter, you have to hit—a lot. Of course you'll get to hit in games, but if you want to get more hitting practice, try these ideas:

umpire: The umpire is the referee of a baseball game, who decides all close calls. Is the pitch a ball or a strike? Is the runner safe or out? Is the ball fair or foul? The umpire's decision is final. A good umpire can make a game much, much more fun: Since the ump makes all the close decisions, instead of spending your time arguing with the other team, you can spend your time playing the game.

- **Take a bucket of balls out to an empty field:** Have a friend pitch them all to you. Pick up all the balls, and then you pitch them all to your friend.
- **Get some whiffle balls:** Whiffle balls are plastic balls with holes in them. Since they won't go far, and they are less likely to hurt someone or something than a real baseball, whiffle balls are good for playing on a less spacious field.
- **Hit balls off a tee:** You can practice hitting the ball in different directions: try hitting 10 balls to left field, then 10 to center field, then 10 to right field.
- **Go to a batting cage.**

Hitting Practice Is the Time to Experiment

Try out different kinds of bats—heavy bats, light bats, long bats, short bats, wooden bats, and metal bats. You don't necessarily have to buy yourself a brand-new bat to try it out. Ask to borrow a bat from a friend, or buy a cheap used bat at a secondhand store.

Then try different ways to stand. Mimic your favorite player's stance. Try out some of the advice a coach or a friend gave you. Find out what feels the most comfortable. As long as you can see the ball well, as long as you can "keep your eye on the ball" when you make contact, then your stance is fine. You may fine-tune it someday, but for now, go with what feels the best.

Most importantly, work on making contact with the ball. Don't worry about how hard you hit it, don't swing hard to hit home runs, just practice *hitting* the ball with every swing. After all this hitting practice, you'll find your hitting in games to be more consistent. Your body will know exactly what to do. You'll end up getting on base a lot; eventually, without even trying, you'll start hitting the ball harder.

Defense

The team that isn't batting is called the defense. Their job is to field the ball and put the batters out. The nine players on defense play the different positions described in the list below. Each position requires slightly different skills, though all defensive players must be able to throw well.

- **Infielders:** Those who play first base, second base, third base, and shortstop are called infielders. Infielders play close to the batter and to the bases. They field ground balls and try to throw out the batter. When a ball is hit into the outfield, the infielders receive the ball from the outfielders and try to tag out runners.
- **Outfielders:** The right fielder, left fielder, and center fielder are the outfielders. They play far away from the batter and the bases. Their main job is to catch fly balls and to throw the ball back to the infielders.
- **Catcher:** The catcher crouches behind home plate to catch any pitch that the batter doesn't hit. If a runner tries to steal a base, the catcher tries to throw the runner out.
- **Pitcher:** The pitcher starts all the action on the field by throwing every pitch to the batter. Pitchers also have to field ground balls and help out the infielders.

The best way to improve your baseball skills is to play in lots of games. A fielder needs to develop a "baseball sense" in addition to physical skills. This means not just being able to field and throw the ball, but knowing *where* to throw the ball, and where to be on the field. When you're in the field, think to yourself before every pitch: If the ball comes to me, what do I do with it? If the ball doesn't come to me, where am I supposed to go?

WORDS to KNOW

choking up: Sometimes a coach will suggest that you "choke up" on the bat. This means to hold your hands higher above the end of the bat, as you can see in the picture below. Choking up makes it easier to contact the ball, but more difficult to hit the ball hard.

WORDS to KNOW

ghost runner: You can play baseball with as few as two or three players per team. But let's say that a three-player team loads the bases. The next batter is standing on third base! What do you do? You put a "ghost runner" on third. The other runners run the bases as normal, but everyone pretends that the ghost runner is running, too. You should make rules ahead of time about how to put a ghost runner out!

By answering these questions before every pitch in every game you play, you will build up good baseball instincts that you may not even be aware of. You'll find yourself making great plays simply because you knew what to do before the batter even hit the ball.

Often, though, you may not have a game to play in; so here are some ways to practice your defensive skills.

Throwing

The most important defensive skill, regardless of position, is throwing. Everyone on the field needs to be able to throw accurately over short and long distances.

How do you get good at throwing? Practice. Find a friend, grab your gloves, and play catch. Don't necessarily throw as hard as you can, or as far as you can; just stand at a comfortable distance, and practice throwing the ball right to your friend. For example, see how many throws you can make to each other without dropping the ball. Once you can make thirty or forty throws in a row, each of you take a big step back, and try again.

A way to practice throwing by yourself is to find a heavy, solid wall, like the backboard at a tennis or handball court. Use chalk to lightly mark a square about chest high. Using a tennis ball, try to hit the wall inside the square. You can design a game—call a "strike" if the ball hits inside the square, call a "ball" if the ball hits on the line or outside the square. Try to earn a strikeout by throwing three strikes before you throw four balls. Once strikeouts become easy, take a step back and try again, or redraw a smaller square.

Fielding Ground Balls

When the batter hits a ground ball, the infielders try to pick up the ball, then throw to first base quickly to put the batter out.

When developing your skill at fielding ground balls, don't worry at first about making the throw to first base. Start by making sure you can catch the ball every time. Shuffle your feet to get your body in front of the ball; watch the ball all the way until it is inside your glove. Try to be in such a good position that anytime the ball takes a funny hop it hits you in the leg or in the chest and stops nearby. That way you'll still be able to pick the ball up quickly.

The way to get good at fielding grounders is (surprise!) to practice. Set up some bases with a couple of friends. Put one person at bat, one person at first base, and one person at shortstop. Have the batter hit ground balls toward the shortstop, who should field them and throw to first base. Keep this up until the shortstop successfully fields five or ten balls in a row; then rotate who gets to play shortstop. Two friends can also roll grounders to each other. You can even practice grounders by throwing a tennis ball against a wall, and fielding the rebound.

Catching Fly Balls

Outfielders especially have to practice fielding fly balls. The hardest part of catching flies is figuring out where the ball is headed. Once you know where the ball is going to land, run to that spot, turn toward the ball with your glove above your head, and catch the ball in front of you.

FUN FACT

Even Major Leaguers Practice

A story is told that one time, the great San Diego hitter Tony Gwynn didn't get a hit in a game that lasted almost until midnight. On his way home, Gwynn stopped by his old high school, where he had a key to the batting cage. He practiced hitting in the cage for about an hour before he went to bed.

WORDS to KNOW

pull hitter: A right-handed pull hitter tends to hit the ball to left field every time. (Of course, a left-handed pull hitter tends to hit to right field.) Pull hitters usually generate a lot of power, but they are easy to defend against. The best hitters can also hit to the opposite field, in other words, right field for a right-handed hitter.

Try not to have to catch a ball while you're still running—this makes it harder to judge where the ball is, so it's more likely you'll drop it; also, if you're running, the throw back to the infield will be harder to make. Of course, sometimes a ball is hit so far away from you that the only way to catch it is to keep running as hard as you can the whole way. But if you can manage to stop before you catch the ball, do it.

Fly ball practice is best done with a real batter, not just with someone throwing the ball in the air. Try to get friends to hit fly balls to you, especially if you have some friends who are good batters. Often, though, high school kids or adults can give the best fly ball practice, because they might have better bat control to hit a lot of good fly balls.

ADVICE FROM THE BEST

Cobb on Hitting

Ty Cobb was one of the best hitters ever. He recommended that hitters not hold the bat all the way at the bottom. He suggested holding the hands an inch from the knob, and to keep the hands an inch apart from each other for better balance and bat control. Not everyone should hit this way; but Ty Cobb had a career .367 batting average and made the Hall of Fame, so perhaps he gave good advice.

Pitching

In the major leagues, pitchers are specialists—that is, their job is only to pitch, and they rarely work on any other skills or play any other positions. Major-league pitchers spend their practice time building arm and leg strength, practicing different types of pitches, and resting their arms.

When younger people play baseball, however, the pitcher is just a good player who can throw the ball accurately. Pitchers who aren't pitching usually play elsewhere in the field.

It is far, far more important for a pitcher to be able to hit a target than for a pitcher to throw hard, or to throw different pitches.

Professional pitchers throw 80, 90, or even 100 miles per hour; they throw curveballs, knuckleballs, sliders, and forkballs. But they are *professionals*. They are pitching to the best hitters in the world, so they must take every advantage.

Why do hitters like night baseball?

Connect the dots to find the answer to the above riddle.

Because there are more

to choose from!

FUN FACT

Little League Facts

Little League baseball began in 1939 in Williamsport, Pennsylvania, where the Little League World Series is still played today. Little League baseball is popular with boys and girls of all ages, and from all over the world—the Little League World Series includes lots of teams from outside the United States. Teams usually have between 12 and 20 players on them, and everyone on a team should get a chance to play.

The best youth league and even high school pitchers don't necessarily throw hard or curvy stuff. They throw a fastball consistently to the catcher's glove every time, whether the catcher asks for a pitch inside or outside, high or low.

What kind of pitch can you throw besides a fastball? Try a changeup. You normally grip a fastball with your thumb and your first two fingers. Instead, try holding the ball all the way back in your palm, but use the same motion as you do for a fastball. You should find that this pitch goes just a bit slower; that's a changeup. Changeups are hard to hit because they throw off the batter's timing—the batter will start to swing just before the ball gets to the plate. If you can throw just a fastball and changeup, and if you can throw them right to the catcher's glove on every pitch, then you will be an outstanding young pitcher.

Fun Baseball Alternatives

If you're short on players or equipment but you really want to get a game of baseball in, don't panic! There are a few alternatives that are similar to baseball that you can play when you only have a few friends available or you can't get your hands on a bat, ball, or glove.

Punchball

This game uses the same basic idea of baseball, but if you don't have gloves, bats, or a field handy, you can use a tennis ball, or even a heavy wad of taped-up paper. Throw the ball up above your head, then swing your extended arm like a bat and "punch" the ball. Position as many fielders as you have at bases and in the outfield.

Curve Ball

The curve ball is one of the trickiest pitches to hit. See if you can score by running a line of color through each of the curvy baseball terms in the following list! Instead of reading in a straight line, each word has one bend in it. Words can go in any direction.

HINT: One word has been done for you.

ASTROTURF

BLEACHERS

DUGOUT

HOMERUN

HOTDOG

POP FLY

SCOREBOARD

SHORTSTOP

STADIUM

WORLD SERIES

```
F L Y L E B O A R D T O
U P O R R L E R N P O P
G R O M F E S E I R E S
A C U P D A T S C T M D
S S T G I C O S H I R L
T K R U U H N D S N R
R B O E M O R E P U T O
I O U S R H O T R S G W
H O T T S T O P E S O O
O M D U U H O T M T U B
T D O L R K M M O A T L
R O G D B F E O H D M A
```

You don't need a pitcher or a catcher, and if you don't have enough people to fill the other positions, you can shrink the field and only play with three bases and two out-fielders (it's often hard to punch a ball to the outfield, any-way). Punchball is a good alternative to baseball or softball if you're looking for a baseball-like game to play with a few friends.

Two-Ball

This is a good baseball game for six to eight total players. Divide the players into pairs. Each pair takes a turn at bat while everyone else plays in the field. A pitcher pitches to a batter as in normal baseball. The batter hits the ball and runs to first . . . but the batter is out if any fielder can touch the ball before the batter reaches first base. The batter's partner then bats. The batting pair doesn't run the bases: base runners are ghost runners who advance whenever the batter gets a hit. After the batters make three outs, they go into the field, and the next pair comes in to bat. This is a fun but exhausting game. On offense, it will help you develop your ability to hit the ball where you want it to go; defenders will develop their range. Oh, and playing this game will help make sure you're in shape!

FUN FACT

Other "Little" Leagues

Even if you're not ready for official Little League ball, you might have other options. In "tee ball," there's no pitcher—the batter just hits the ball off a tee. Other leagues allow coaches to pitch to the players or limit each inning to nine batters. Ask around to find out what kinds of leagues for young players are available in your community.

Chapter 2
The History of Baseball

There are 30 major-league teams today, and many more minor league teams with players hoping to make it to the big leagues. There are thousands of college teams, high school teams, and little league teams all playing baseball. But where did it all begin? How did the major leagues get started? This chapter will answer all your questions!

The Earliest Games

No one is quite sure who actually invented baseball. Some people believe that in 1839, when Abner Doubleday began playing a game called "town ball" in Cooperstown, New York, baseball was born. Other people, however, give credit to Alexander Cartwright, who in the early 1840s developed a game played on a diamond-shaped field with rules that resemble those we know. These early games were based on the games Cricket and Rounders, both played in England. Either way, Doubleday and Cartwright are both in their own ways given credit for beginning the game we love today.

On June 19, 1846, at Elysian Fields in Hoboken, New Jersey, the first organized and recorded baseball game took place. Two amateur teams from New York City, the Knickerbockers and the New York Nine, played a four-inning game, won by the Nine, 23 to 1. Pitchers threw underhanded, no one had gloves, the ball was softer than what we know as a baseball today, and the bases were 42 paces (probably about 120 feet) from each other—but it was baseball. The idea was to hit the ball, get from base to base safely, and score runs before getting three outs in your team's turn at bat.

FUN FACT

Vintage Base Ball

You can still watch Base Ball (as it was called in the mid-1800s) in its vintage form. For example, the Elizabeth Resolutes, based in Elizabeth, New Jersey, play 13 games or so a year in which they dress in authentic 1800s uniforms and play by 1800s rules.

From that first game, baseball caught on quickly. Amateur teams were formed, and they played until the first team scored 21 runs, which at that time only took a few innings. In 1857 the idea of playing a nine-inning game was introduced, the bases were placed 90 feet apart, and more rules were changed. The 1850s was also the time when a writer named Henry Chadwick became the first baseball editor, writing about baseball, promoting the game, and inventing the box score that is still in newspapers (and on the Internet) today. By the time the Civil War broke out in 1861, baseball was being played all over the country. Soldiers played the game during the war, making further changes to the rules. Around this time the idea of calling a ball for a bad pitch was introduced, and stealing a base also became part of the game.

The First Professional Teams

As far back as the 1860s there were barnstorming teams, which were teams that went from city to city playing each other. The first of these teams to be made up entirely of paid players was the Cincinnati Red Stockings of 1869. The record of that first professional team was 57–0. In 1871 the National Association of Professional Baseball Players was formed with nine teams. The Philadelphia Athletics were the first champions, winning twenty-two and losing only seven. By 1875 too much gambling caused people to lose interest in this league, but not in baseball. In 1876 the National League was formed. Many players from the original association became part of this new league, including "Cap" Anson, who was considered one of the game's first star players.

box score: A box score is a grid containing a summary of each player's game statistics. Take a look at Chapter 8 to learn how to read a box score.

FUN FACT

The Curse of the Bambino

Between 1903 and 1918, the Boston Red Sox won the World Series five times. Following the 1919 season, the Red Sox traded Babe Ruth ("the Bambino") to the New York Yankees. After the trade, the Red Sox didn't win another World Series for 86 years. They lost in the deciding game of the playoffs or World Series on six occasions. This misfortune is called the "Curse of the Bambino."

WORDS to KNOW

World Series: The winners of the National League and the American League have played the World Series each fall since 1903 (with two exceptions). You can read about its history and greatest moments in Chapter 6.

Through the 1880s and 1890s, several other leagues, including the American Association, the Players League, and a minor league called the Western League, began. All failed except for the Western League.

The National League, however, was a big success.

Baseball Through the Decades

The "Modern Era" of baseball is said to have begun in 1900. Here is a look at what happened in baseball history in each of the decades of the 1900s and in the current century.

1900–1909

World Championships: Cubs 2, Boston Americans, New York Giants, White Sox, Pirates

Most famous players: Honus Wagner, Nap Lajoie, Ty Cobb, Cy Young, Christy Mathewson

In 1901 the Western League turned into the American League and started taking players from the National League. National League (NL) team owners were not too happy about this. The unfriendliness between the two leagues lasted for two years, until they finally united in 1903 and created the concept of a World Series between the two leagues.

The first decade of the 1900s featured a great Chicago Cubs team that in 1906 won 116 games and lost only 36. They played in three World Series and won two of them. The Cubs featured an incredible infield combination that included Joe Tinker at shortstop, John Evers at second base, and Frank Chance at first base.

Nap Lajoie was the American League's first batting champion, with an incredible .422 batting average, topped only once ever since. Ty Cobb and Honus Wagner were great hitters and had tremendous speed, stealing plenty of bases. Pitching was very different then: there were only five or six pitchers on a team, and starters pitched more often and for more innings than they do today. Hitters hit plenty of singles, doubles, and even triples, but home runs were not common, and league leaders did not top 16 homers through 1910.

1910–1919

World Championships: Red Sox 4, Philadelphia A's 3, Boston Braves, White Sox, Reds

Most famous players: Ty Cobb, Tris Speaker, Gavvy Cravath, Walter Johnson, Joe Jackson

The United States was immersed in the First World War during the latter part of this decade. Yet baseball continued uninterrupted. The major leagues were challenged by a new league called the Federal League, which spent a couple of

FUN FACT

Black Sox

In 1919 the Chicago White Sox earned the name "Black Sox." Eight players on the team were accused of being paid by gamblers to intentionally lose the series to the Reds. The first commissioner of baseball banned the eight players from the game forever. One of those players, "Shoeless" Joe Jackson, was one of baseball's all-time greatest hitters, but because he was kicked out of baseball, Jackson is not eligible for election to the Hall of Fame.

FUN FACT

Who Says Baseball Is a Slow Game?

World Series games in the first decade of the 1900s usually took about an hour and a half. That's amazing, considering that even regular season games today take close to three hours to play.

years taking players away from the American and National Leagues. Finally the major leagues were able to reach an agreement with this new league, which was dissolved. John McGraw, one of baseball's all-time great managers, led the NL's New York Giants to four World Series, but no championships. In the American League, the Philadelphia Athletics, led by their great manager Connie Mack, and the Boston Red Sox were the toughest teams.

Stealing Bases

These teams are some of the first baseball teams in this country! Some are still around, while some have moved to different cities and changed their names. See if you can finish the teams' names by adding the missing letters **B-A-S-E-S.**

```
__LTIMOR_ ORIOL__
_O_TON R_D _OX
N_W YORK M_T_
_ROOKLYN DODG_R_
LO_ _NG_LE_ _NG_L_
_TL_NT_ _R_VE_
```

Walter Johnson won 20 or more games every year in this decade. He was truly a great pitcher. But pitching was certainly easier back in this "dead-ball era." Until about 1920, the ball was much squishier than the baseballs we play with today, and the same ball was usually used for the entire game. Gavvy Cravath of the Phillies led the National League in home runs six times—but he never hit more than 24 homers in a season.

1920–1929

World Championships: Yankees 3, New York Giants 2, Indians, Washington Senators, Pirates, Cardinals, Philadelphia A's

Most famous players: Rogers Hornsby, Babe Ruth, Lou Gehrig, Lefty Grove, Grover Alexander

After World War I, the country entered a period called the Roaring Twenties, filled with plenty of singing, dancing, and great baseball. The most popular player was "The Babe," who was a big hero everywhere he went and the first player to make as much as $50,000, which in those days was a very high salary—equivalent to at least half a million dollars in today's money. The Yankees began their 40-year domination of the major leagues, during which they won 29 American League pennants and 20 world championships.

FUN FACT

Murderer's Row

The greatest lineup in baseball history is thought to be the 1927 lineup of the New York Yankees, nicknamed "Murderer's Row." Here are the season stats of some of their best players. As you look at these, remember that in 1927 only five players hit more than 20 home runs and that 100 RBIs has always been considered to be a very good season. These guys were incredible!

Position	Name	AVG	HR	RBI
1B	Lou Gehrig	.373	47	175
2B/3B/ss	Tony Lazzeri	.309	18	102
LF	Bob Meusel	.337	8	103
CF	Earle Combs	.356	6	64
RF	Babe Ruth	.356	60	164

Uniform Numbers

The Yankees were the first team to wear numbers on their backs in the 1920s. They started out by assigning numbers based on the batting order: Babe Ruth always hit third, so he was number 3. Lou Gehrig always hit fourth, so he was number 4, and so on. Today the number on a player's uniform is only used to identify the player, and has nothing to do with where the player bats.

FUN FACT

Retired Numbers

A team will sometimes "retire" the number of a famous player. This means that no one else on that team ever wears the retired number again—for example, the Cincinnati Reds retired Johnny Bench's number 5, so a Reds uniform with 5 on it will forever be associated with Bench. The Yankees have retired 16 different uniform numbers, the most of any team.

Travel by Train

Today, most teams get from one city to the other in a few hours by private jet. Through much of baseball's history, though, teams took trains on their road trips. That's the main reason why there were no major-league teams in the west or the south—a trip just from New York to Chicago meant sitting (and sleeping) on the train for an entire day.

The dead-ball era was over in the 1920s. Though many sluggers emerged, it was Babe Ruth who captured the imagination of the fans. His record of 60 homers in 1927 stood for 34 years; his 714 career home runs were the most ever until 1974. Whether it was because of all the home runs or not, baseball reached enormous popularity in the 1920s. In 1928, 61,000 people came to Yankee Stadium to watch the Yankees defeat the Cardinals in Game 1 of the World Series; nearly 40,000 attended Game 3 in the much smaller city of St. Louis. Baseball cemented its role as the national pastime.

1930–1939

World Championships: Yankees 5, Cardinals 2, Philadelphia A's, New York Giants, Tigers

Most famous players: Lefty Grove, Lou Gehrig, Johnny Mize, Jimmie Foxx, Hack Wilson, Dizzy Dean

Times were difficult for many Americans in the 1930s because of the Great Depression. Many people were out of work and without much money. Baseball was still something to turn to for fun and to forget about the tough times. Jimmy Foxx of the Philadelphia A's came close to Ruth's home run record, hitting 58 homers in one season. The Cubs' Hack Wilson set a one-season record that still holds today, driving in 191 runs. Babe Ruth played his last game for the Yankees in 1934, and then played a few with the Braves in 1935 before retiring. Ruth's teammate Lou Gehrig continued to play alongside a new teammate who appeared in 1936, another baseball legend named Joe DiMaggio. Gehrig retired because of a serious illness in 1937 after playing in 2,130 consecutive games, a record that many thought would never be broken.

Another lasting change to the game took place in 1935 in Cincinnati when the first night game was played. The idea caught on fast, and pretty soon many night games would appear on the schedule—except at Wrigley Field in Chicago, where night games were not played until 1988.

1940–1949

World Championships: Yankees 4, Cardinals 3, Reds, Tigers, Indians

Most famous players: Warren Spahn, Johnny Sain, Ted Williams, Joe DiMaggio, Bob Feller

World War II was the country's main focus in the first half of the 1940s, and many ballplayers left their teams to serve in the United States military. Young players and veterans who were too old for the military made up most of the teams. Since many of the men were in the army, women's baseball teams emerged, attracting a lot of attention as they played in their own league. The movie *A League of Their Own* is based on this 1940s women's baseball league.

Even though most American young people were off to war, baseball remained an important part of their lives. Soldiers were proud of their hometown teams, and they kept track as best they could of events in the major leagues. The infantrymen even used baseball questions to distinguish friend from foe. They say that General Omar Bradley once failed to convince a lookout that he was an American soldier, because he didn't know that the Brooklyn Dodgers played in the National League.

Youngest Player Ever

In 1944, when most of the country's young men were involved in the war effort, 15-year-old Joe Nuxhall pitched in a game for the Cincinnati Reds to become the youngest major leaguer ever. Nuxhall was quickly sent back down to the minor leagues. But he rejoined the Reds in 1952 and played in the majors for 15 years. Nuxhall returned to the Reds in 1967 as a broadcaster. His was the radio voice of the Reds for four decades, until his death in 2007.

Spahn and Sain

Warren Spahn and Johnny Sain led the pitching staff of the 1948 Boston Braves. Manager Billy Southworth wished he could let them pitch every day. So Gerald V. Hern of the *Boston Post* wrote a poem about them. The poem "Spahn and Sain and Pray for Rain" lives on in baseball's collective memory as nearly a motto for the '48 Braves.

Hard Ball

Baseball is a game full of action! Fill in as many wild words as you can, using the across and down clues. We left you some T-O-U-G-H letters and words as hints!

ACROSS

3. Fun baseball game played against an upright surface.

6. Team name: Pittsburgh _____

7. Nickname for a powerful hitter.

11. Smooth, round stick used to hit a baseball.

13. The 37 foot high wall in Boston's Fenway Park.

16. A "_____ hitter" is a hitter who hits for someone else.

17. To run from one base to another before the next player at bat has hit the ball.

19. Team Name: San Francisco _____.

21. If the hitter bunts with a man on third base, it's called a "_____ play."

DOWN

1. Joe DiMaggio's nickname: "_____ 'n Joe."

2. When a hitter stops getting hits for a while.

4. Hank Aaron's nickname: "The _____".

5. "The _____" is when fans stand and then sit while moving their arms up and down in a motion that goes all around the stadium."

6. A "_____" fly goes high up in the air and is easily caught.

7. Sharp bumps on the bottom of baseball player's shoes.

8. "The Seventh Inning _____" gives fan a chance to get up and move around.

9. Team name: Los Angeles _____.

10. The score made by a player who touches first, second, third, and home base.

11. Jose Conseco and Mark McGwire were known as the "_____ Brothers."

12. A ball hit out of fair territory.

14. A _____ play is when a player is trapped between two bases. He has to scramble to get to one base or the other before being tagged out.

15. A "_____ ball" is the speediest pitch.

18. A player will sometimes have to _____ headfirst into a base to avoid being tagged out.

20. A "grand_____" is a home run hit when bases are loaded.

SLUMP

BAT

POP

DIVE   SLUGGER   JOLT

HAMMER

BASH   SLAM

23

Rookie of the Year

Since 1947 with Jackie Robinson, the best first-year player in each league has been honored with the Rookie of the Year award.

Why Brooklyn?

New York City consists of five large sections called boroughs. Unlike the Yankees and Giants, the Dodgers claimed to represent only one of these five boroughs, Brooklyn. But Brooklyn by itself was larger than any other American city except for Chicago!

Most soldiers returned from the war in 1945 and 1946, and the best athletes went into (or back into) major-league baseball. Ted Williams, Joe DiMaggio, and Bob Feller were among the most well-known baseball and military heroes of the day. Williams in particular had already established himself as a great hitter, batting .406 in 1941. No one has batted over .400 since then. Though he took three years off from baseball, Williams returned to the game in 1946 and batted over .300 every year until 1959.

Winning World War II required a full effort from all segments of American society. Afterward, many thought it ridiculous that, for example, black folks were allowed to risk their lives in battle, but were (among other things) not allowed to play major-league baseball. Many great players, including Jackie Robinson, Cool Papa Bell, Josh Gibson, and Satchel Paige played in the Negro Leagues (see the section later in this chapter). There were many great players in these leagues, a number of whom would have been big stars in the major leagues if only the team owners would have let them play. In 1947, well before the significant civil rights movement of the 1960s, Brooklyn Dodgers general manager Branch Rickey promoted Jackie Robinson to the majors, thus breaking the "color line" and paving the way for the thorough integration of professional baseball over the next decades.

The Negro Leagues

The National League was formed in 1876, and in the early years of baseball people of any race could play. In fact, Moses Fleetwood joined the Toledo ball club in 1884 as the first black professional ballplayer, and others followed. These players, however, were treated badly by fans, opposing players, and their own teammates. Besides calling them names, white pitchers would often throw knockdown pitches at them. Little by little, as 1900 approached, there were fewer and fewer black players in baseball. There was no written rule, but owners just no longer signed black players. Such informal yet real discrimination was typical in most parts of American society in the first part of the 20th century.

Since it was becoming impossible to get into the major leagues, black players (referred to in those days as Negroes) began forming their own teams in the 1890s. By the early 1900s these teams were playing independently all over the eastern part of the United States in cities like New York and Philadelphia. Often these teams played exhibition games against major-league teams, and they did well. It was obvious that many of the players on these teams had the talent to play in the major leagues, but the practice of discrimination by race was too strong, and they did not break into the all-white major leagues.

One great pitcher of the early 1900s was Rube Foster, who pitched for the 1906 Philadelphia Giants. He went on to be the founder of the "Negro Leagues," which began in 1920 with eight teams. In 1923, Foster helped start a second league, which began with six new teams.

Negro Leagues faced major problems, such as finding places to play. Often the teams had to rent stadiums from white owners, who didn't always treat them fairly. Many owners did not allow them to use the "white" locker rooms. Nonetheless, the teams persisted, with players playing for the love of the game more than anything else, since most were not making much money.

The 1930s, however, marked the end of the early Negro Leagues because of the Depression, during which

WORDS to KNOW

pennant: The team that represents the National League or the American League in the World Series is said to have won the pennant.

ADVICE FROM THE BEST

Paige on Age

Negro Leagues star and former major-league pitcher Satchel Paige, who pitched for nearly 30 years and even appeared in a major-league game at the age of 59, once said, "Age is a case of mind over matter. If you don't mind, it don't matter."

virtually all Americans were poor by today's standards. Most of the teams, which had a hard time making money, had to call it quits. There were, however, some teams that managed to play—touring teams such as the Pittsburgh Crawfords and Washington, D.C.'s Homestead Grays. Many major leaguers had great respect for the black ballplayers and still played exhibition games against these touring teams. By the late 1930s, as the country's economy improved, the Negro Leagues were back with new teams.

In the 1940s a team in Brooklyn, the Brooklyn Brown Bombers, was owned by Dodgers president and general manager Branch Rickey. Rickey was determined, despite the feelings of the other team owners, to scout and sign baseball's first black major leaguer. In 1946 it was Rickey who watched the Kansas City Monarchs come to town with a young player named Jackie Robinson. Rickey signed Robinson to a minor league contract in 1945, and called him up as a member of the Dodgers in 1947.

As more and more black players made the major leagues, there was less of a need for the Negro Leagues. While many of the greatest Negro League stars never made it to the major leagues, the leagues served a purpose in giving these ballplayers a place to show their great talents and play the game they loved. It would eventually serve as a showcase for players to get to the major leagues. One cannot help but wonder how some of the great major leaguers in history might have fared in daily competition against all of the country's best athletes, not just those who happened to be white.

1950–1959

World Championships: Yankees 6, New York Giants, Milwaukee Braves, Brooklyn Dodgers, Los Angeles Dodgers

Most famous players: Willie Mays, Mickey Mantle, Duke Snider, Ted Williams, Whitey Ford, Stan Musial

The city of New York dominated baseball. Their three teams—the Yankees, the Giants, and the Dodgers—were the best in the game, and they competed for the city's attention. One of the most memorable moments from those New York rivalries occurred at the end of the 1951 season. The New York Giants and the Brooklyn Dodgers were tied for first place in the NL, so they played one game to see which team would go to the World Series. The Dodgers led the game 4–1 going into the bottom of the ninth inning. The Giants got one run to make the score 4–2, then Bobby Thompson came to bat against pitcher Ralph Branca with two men on base. Thompson hit a home run to left field, winning the game 5–4 and sending the Giants to the World Series. On

---

The Beloved Bums from Brooklyn

An important way of getting around New York City used to be the trolley, which was a sort of train that ran at street level. People had to dodge the trolleys as they crossed streets—hence, the baseball team became the Brooklyn Trolley Dodgers. But fans sometimes referred to their team simply as the "Bums."

FUN FACT

The Asterisk

When Babe Ruth hit his 60 homers in 1927, teams played 154 games in a season. But in 1961, the American League changed to a 162-game schedule—Roger Maris had eight extra games to beat the Babe's record! Commissioner Ford Frick decreed that Maris's record of 61 homers would be listed with an asterisk indicating the extra games that Maris played.

The Sad History of the Senators

In 1901, the American League's Washington Senators played their first game in the nation's capital. After the 1960 season, they moved to Minneapolis to become the Minnesota Twins. The very next year, a new Washington Senators team began play. But ten years later, these Senators moved to Dallas to become the Texas Rangers! The city of Washington must have learned its lesson. The current Washington team, which started play in 2005, is called the Nationals, not the Senators.

the radio, Giants announcer Russ Hodges conveyed the fans' excitement with his famous call, shouting over and over, "The Giants win the pennant! The Giants win the pennant!" Thompson's home run became known as the "Shot heard round the world."

Americans began commonly using a number of new technologies in the 1950s, including refrigerators, washing machines, transistor radios, and other devices. Two new technologies caused lasting changes in major-league baseball. The first was the beginning of televised baseball. Though today virtually every game can be seen on TV, in the early 1950s most people didn't even own television sets. But by the end of the decade baseball could be seen by millions of people even when they couldn't go to the games.

It was the jet airplane that caused the great New York baseball rivalries to end. By the end of the 1950s, travel by jet was common, meaning that people could get from the country's east coast to the west coast in less than a day. So, in 1958, both the Dodgers and the Giants moved to the west coast—the Dodgers to Los Angeles, the Giants to San Francisco.

1960–1969

World Championships: Yankees 2, Dodgers 2, Cardinals 2, Pirates, Orioles, Tigers, Mets

Most famous players: Bob Gibson, Sandy Koufax, Don Drysdale, Hank Aaron, Frank Robinson, Willie McCovey, Carl Yastrzemski

New York maintained its reign as the focus of the baseball world, as the Yankees played in the World Series in 1960–1964. Yankee outfielder Roger Maris dueled with teammate Mickey Mantle for the 1961 home run crown—Maris hit number 61 on the last day of the season, breaking Babe Ruth's hallowed record.

The 1960s were a time of expansion. The number of teams in each league hadn't changed for many decades. But in 1961, the American League added two new teams, the Los Angeles Angels, and the Washington Senators.

A year later, the National League added two new teams, the New York Mets and the Houston Colt 45s. New teams are usually not very good, but in 1962 the Mets won only 40 games while losing 122 in the new 162-game season. This was the worst record ever, and the Mets were greeted with many appropriate jokes.

The Colt 45s, meanwhile, changed their name to the Astros and moved into a super new stadium called the Astrodome. It was the first indoor stadium, with fake grass called Astroturf and a giant, "modern" scoreboard. The Astrodome was, in the mid-1960s, something that seemed like it came from out of the future.

Baseball expanded by four more teams in 1969: the Montreal Expos and San Diego Padres in the National League, the Seattle Pilots and Kansas City Royals in the American League. The twelve-team leagues were split into two six-team divisions, east and west.

Now you're probably wondering what happened to those terrible Mets. Well, after being pretty dreadful for seven years, they shocked the world in 1969. The same year that people landed on the moon for the first time ever, the Mets beat the Baltimore Orioles in five games to win the World Series.

League Championship Series

Until 1969, whichever team won the most regular-season games in each league went to the World Series. But starting in 1969, the leagues were split into divisions. The League Championship Series, or LCS, was played between the division winners. So today, the ALCS and the NLCS decide which team in each league goes to the World Series.

designated hitter: A designated hitter (DH) is a player who bats for the pitcher. The American League uses the DH, but the National League does not—NL pitchers must bat for themselves.

1970–1979

World Championships: A's 3, Pirates 2, Reds 2, Yankees 2, Orioles

Most famous players: Reggie Jackson, Joe Morgan, Willie Stargell, Tom Seaver, Catfish Hunter, Pete Rose, Johnny Bench

The 1970s is probably the time when your parents first began to follow baseball. Even just 30 years ago, the major leagues were very different than they are today. For one thing, players could not be "free agents." Rather, once a player was assigned to a team, he could not change teams unless he was traded or released. In 1972 the Major League Baseball players went on strike; by 1975 players won the right to free agency.

Games were usually lower-scoring in those days. For example, in the American League in 1970, teams averaged 4.2 runs per game; in 2006, they averaged 5.0 runs per game. Owners wanted to increase scoring. They had already lowered the height of the pitching mound in 1968, from 15 inches high to its current height of 10 inches. So, in 1973 the American League introduced the "designated hitter," to the dismay of all right-thinking baseball fans.

Many teams moved into bigger stadiums in the 1970s, most of which used the same AstroTurf that the Astros put inside their dome. Turf caused the baseball to take high bounces, forcing fielders to adjust their positioning. Speed became a more important part of the game on turf. In 1977 Lou Brock became the first player ever to steal 900 bases, after he broke Ty Cobb's previous record of 892. (Rickey Henderson has since passed them both.) Most of these old stadiums were shaped like enormous concrete circles, and were also used for football, concerts, rodeos, and other big events.

Who Said Pitchers Can't Hit?

In 1942, Jim Tobin hit three home runs in one game. In the 1960s, Tony Clonginger hit two grand slams. No other pitchers have ever equaled these records.

Best Record, No Reward

The team with the best record in the 1981 season was the Cincinnati Reds. However, because of the strike and the split season, they didn't make it to the World Series; they didn't even make it to the playoffs. They finished second to the Dodgers in the first half, and second to the Astros in the second half.

Tickets were much cheaper then than now. In those days, a five-dollar ticket might be considered outrageously expensive, while now, if a five-dollar ticket is available at all, it's as a special discount.

On April 8, 1974, "Hammerin'" Hank Aaron of the Atlanta Braves hit his 715th career home run, one more than Babe Ruth hit. Aaron went on to finish his career where he began it, in Milwaukee, with 755 homers.

1980–1989

World Championships: Dodgers 2, Phillies, Cardinals, Orioles, Tigers, Royals, Mets, Twins, A's.

Most famous players: Ozzie Smith, Nolan Ryan, Dennis Eckersley, Mike Schmidt, George Brett, Wade Boggs, Tony Gwynn, Ricky Henderson

Free agency caused player salaries to increase rapidly. In response, owners tried to limit players' abilities to change teams; as a result, baseball players went on strike in the middle of the 1981 season. Over 700 games were canceled and when baseball finally returned, the season was split into two halves. The winners of the first half played the winners of the second half in a special playoff series. Fans were not happy, and did not watch much baseball on television or at the park in the second part of the 1981 season.

Baseball recovered to play some entertaining seasons. Half of the twenty-six teams played in at least one World Series in the 1980s, and nine different teams won championships. Speed continued to be a critical element of strategy. The St. Louis Cardinals, under manager Whitey Herzog, relied on slick-fielding, singles-hitting speedsters to lead them to three World Series. Ricky Henderson broke the all-time stolen-base record.

FUN FACT

Family Affair

At one time, Cal Ripken Jr. and his brother Billy both played for the Baltimore Orioles, with their dad as coach. In 1987 and 1988 their dad was also the manager.

Champions

ADVICE FROM THE BEST

Mazzone on Pitching

Most starting pitchers are afraid to throw too much between starts for fear of hurting their arms. Braves pitching coach Leo Mazzone thought that was ridiculous. He had his pitchers throw off the mound twice between starts, though only at about half speed. He seemed to know what he was doing, as the Braves had the best starting pitching in the majors for over a decade.

WORDS to KNOW

wild card: The winner of each division earns a spot in the playoffs. But a fourth team in each league also makes the playoffs—the team that has the next-best record in the league after the division winners. This "wild card" team has the same chance to win the World Series as any other playoff team; in fact, four wild card teams have won the championship.

The art of base stealing reached its peak in the 1980s, but the art of relief pitching was only beginning its evolution. Until the 1970s it was normal for the starting pitcher to pitch the whole game. Relief pitchers, whose specific role was to pitch only the late innings, became much more specialized in the 1980s. Most teams began to use a "closer," a relief pitcher with the job of finishing just the last inning or two. Toward the end of the decade, teams began to use "setup" relievers, who relieved the starter in the seventh or eighth inning, but gave way to the closer in the ninth.

1990–1999

World Championships: Yankees 3, Blue Jays 2, Reds, Twins, Braves, Marlins

Most famous players: Greg Maddux, Tom Glavine, John Smoltz, Randy Johnson, Cal Ripken Jr., Barry Bonds, Mark McGwire.

The National League of the 1990s was the Atlanta Braves' League. The Braves, led by pitching coach Leo Mazzone, manager Bobby Cox, general manager John Schuerholz, and their phenomenal starting pitchers, were the most consistently strong team in the league. They won their division every year between 1991 and 2005. They only won one World Series title, though, in 1995 when they beat the Cleveland Indians.

The major leagues expanded even more in the 1990s, with the addition of the Florida Marlins, Colorado Rockies, Arizona Diamondbacks, and Tampa Bay Devil Rays. This brought the number of major-league teams to today's total of thirty. The playoff structure was changed once again in 1994, to the present format. Each league was split into three divisions—east, central, and west.

In 1995, Cal Ripken Jr. of the Orioles set a record by playing in his 2,131st consecutive game, breaking the record set by Lou Gehrig in 1939. The September 6 game drew a sellout crowd, which included the president of the United States, plus millions of fans who watched on TV around the world. Ripken ended his streak in 1998, after 2,632 consecutive games played.

In one of the saddest episodes in baseball history, a strike ended the 1994 baseball season in August. It was the first time since 1904 that there was no postseason, no World Series, and no championship team. Millionaire players and millionaire team owners got very little sympathy from the fans, who were deprived of watching and enjoying their favorite game. When baseball returned in 1995, attendance was way down. For the next couple of seasons many fans were turned off to baseball.

In 1997 baseball owners decided that they'd try to draw fans back by starting interleague play, which meant regular season games between National and American league teams. Longtime baseball fans weren't happy about it, but on June 12, 1997, the Texas Rangers and San Francisco Giants played in the first interleague game. What at first appeared to be a novelty caught on as crosstown rivals like the Cubs and White Sox in Chicago, the A's and Giants in neighboring Oakland and San Francisco, and the Mets and Yankees in New York all faced each other during the season.

Starting in the mid-1990s, players hit more home runs than ever before. Back in 1983, Mike Schmidt hit 40 home runs to lead the league. In 1996, though, 40 home runs was only good for 12th best in the majors. In 1998, not just one, but two players hit more home runs in the season than ever before. Sammy

FUN FACT

The Minor Leagues

Each major-league team supports several minor-league teams, which played even through the strike of 1994. Almost every player spends a few years in the minors before coming to the major leagues. Some players are sent back down to the minor leagues if they are not playing well, and sometimes good major-league players will go to the minors after an injury to get used to playing again. Minor-league teams are in many smaller cities across the country.

Generations

Imagine playing in the major leagues just like your father and your grandfather. Three times it has been done. One family is still going strong today. The Boone family has included major leaguers Ray Boone, his son Bob Boone, and his two grandsons Brett and Aaron Boone.

Sosa hit 66, and Mark McGwire hit 70, both breaking the single season record of 61 held by Roger Maris since 1961.

Several possible reasons for this offensive explosion have been proposed. For one thing, players took weight training more seriously than ever before. In the 1980s, many teams did not even own their own weight rooms—players on the road had to find a local gym if they wanted to work out. But by the '90s, teams built gyms, hired athletic trainers, and reaped the benefits of regular workouts. A second possible reason for more home runs was expansion—the addition of four new teams meant that more than forty pitchers who previously weren't good enough to play in the majors were now pitching to the world's best power hitters.

But much later, in the early 2000s, it came to light that many players were using illegal drugs called anabolic steroids to build their muscles. Sluggers Ken Caminiti and Jose Canseco came forward to tell of their own steroid use and to warn that many others were also using the same drugs. No other players directly admitted to using steroids. However, Barry Bonds was investigated by the FBI; Mark McGwire and Sammy Sosa were called to testify before Congress about their own steroid use. It's still not clear exactly which players were using steroids. But in 2005, the major leagues instituted steroid testing for all players.

2000–2007

World Championships: Red Sox 2, Yankees, Diamondbacks, Angels, Marlins, White Sox, Cardinals

Most famous players: Pedro Martinez, Johan Santana, Manny Ramirez, Albert Pujols, David Ortiz, Ichiro Suzuki, Derek Jeter

The terrorist attacks of 2001 put a halt to baseball, but only for a week. The sport, and especially the 2001 World Series in New York City, served as a rallying event for American culture. Since 2001, many teams have replaced the traditional singing of "Take Me Out to the Ball Game" during the seventh-inning stretch with "God Bless America."

The Chicago Cubs haven't won a World Series since 1908; the Boston Red Sox hadn't won since 1918. Both teams have been considered to be cursed for as long as most people can remember. In 2003, both teams were very good, and both seemed to have a good chance to make the World Series. But in the playoffs, both faltered in memorable fashion. The Cubs were one game away from beating the Florida Marlins in the National League Championship Series, and they were leading the Marlins late in the game. But a Cubs fan reached into the field and interfered with a Cubs player trying to make a catch; that, some timely Marlins hits, and a Cubs error allowed the Marlins to win the game and, the next night, the series. The Red Sox took the Yankees to extra innings in the seventh and final game of the American League Championship Series. But on the first pitch of the Yankees' 13th inning, third baseman Aaron Boone hit a walk-off home run. The cursed teams were still cursed.

The Red Sox earned their revenge in the 2004 ALCS. Though they fell behind to the Yankees three games to none, the Sox came all the way back to win four games to three. Then, they swept the St. Louis Cardinals to win their first World Series in 86 years.

Perhaps the biggest way baseball has changed in the new century is in its national exposure. When your parents were growing up, it was possible to see the home team on television, and one or two other "games of the week." That was it. In the 1990s, cable television allowed people to watch a bit

Following a Game on the Internet

Several sites, including MLB.com, allow you to see the status of a game as it happens. Free applets show who's at bat, who's pitching, lineups, a live box score, and much more.

The Nasty Boys

The Reds of the 1990s used a combination of outstanding relief pitchers. Randy Myers, Rob Dibble, and Norm Charlton regularly held late-inning Reds leads. Two of these three "Nasty Boys," Dibble and Myers, were named most valuable player (MVP) of the 1990 NLCS.

more baseball. But now it is possible to see every game every night using satellite television. Every radio broadcast can be heard on satellite radio. The Internet allows instant access to box scores and stories about every game that is played. Fantasy baseball (see Chapter 10) is growing in popularity, once again due to the Internet.

Even though the game continues to evolve, baseball is still fundamentally the same game that your parents and grandparents watched and played when they were your age. Ask them what stories they have about baseball history; they might be thrilled to tell you about the players and the teams they used to watch. And savor the games you watch now. Some day your own grandchildren might be asking you about your favorite baseball memories.

Ball Clubs on the Move

Many of today's major-league teams played in other cities or had different names in the past. The following is a list of just some of the former names and former homes of the teams we know today.

- The **Oakland Athletics** (also called the A's) had two previous homes. They played in Kansas City from 1955 to 1967, and before that they were the Philadelphia Athletics.
- The **New York Yankees** were known as the Highlanders from 1903 to 1912. Before the American League was officially started, they played in Baltimore as the Baltimore Orioles in 1901 and 1902. The Orioles we know today weren't around then.
- The **Minnesota Twins** were the Washington Senators from 1901 to 1960. After they moved, a new Washington Senators team was formed in 1961; but it moved to become the Texas Rangers.

The History of Baseball

- The **Montreal Expos** played half their home games in San Juan, Puerto Rico in 2003 and 2004. Then they moved to Washington, D.C. to become the Washington Nationals.
- The **Cleveland Indians** were always in Cleveland. However, between 1901 and 1914 they kept changing their name. They were the Blues, the Broncos, and the Naps before becoming the Indians in 1915.
- The **Boston Red Sox**, like the Indians, never moved, but had a hard time finding a name they liked. Between 1901 and 1906 they were known as the Somersets, the Pilgrims, and the Puritans before becoming the Red Sox in 1907.
- The **Baltimore Orioles** that we know today came into being in 1955 after moving from St. Louis, where they were the Browns from 1902 through 1954.

Clever T-shirt

When the Angels made their second name change in just a few years, deciding to call themselves the Los Angeles Angels of Anaheim, the Dodgers decided to have a bit of fun at the Angels expense. They printed T-shirts that said "Los Angeles Dodgers of Los Angeles."

- The **Atlanta Braves** have a long history dating back to 1876 and covering three cities. Prior to moving to Atlanta, they were the Milwaukee Braves from 1953 to 1965. Before that they were in Boston for fifty-nine years. There they were the Red Caps, the Beaneaters, the Doves, and on two different occasions the Bees.
- The **Reds**, the first professional team, were originally known as the Red Stockings. They became the Reds as far back as 1880. They changed their name briefly to the Red Legs in the 1950s. Realizing how silly that sounded, they went back to the Reds.
- The **Los Angeles Dodgers** were the Brooklyn Dodgers until 1957, and they had been known as the Robins from 1914 to 1931.
- The **San Francisco Giants** were the New York Giants until 1957.
- The **Houston Astros** were the Houston Colt 45s for their first three seasons, from 1962 to 1964.
- The **Milwaukee Brewers** were the Seattle Pilots in 1969 before moving to Milwaukee in their second season. In 1997 they also moved from the American to the National League.
- The **Philadelphia Phillies** changed their name to the Blue Jays for the 1944 and 1945 seasons before changing it back to the Phillies.
- The **Angels** play in Anaheim, which is near Los Angeles, California. For years the team was known as the California Angels. They changed to the Anaheim Angels, then to their current extra long name: the Los Angeles Angels of Anaheim.

Professional baseball has existed for well over a century. Part of the charm of the game is discussing and comparing players from different eras. Listed below are some of the best players in baseball history. This list cannot be complete—your or your parents' favorite player from years past might not be listed here. But the Baseball Hall of Fame, discussed in the next chapter, has a more thorough list of the greatest players. Reading this chapter is a great way to start learning about some of baseball's most famous players.

Pitchers

Over the years, there have been changes in pitching in the major leagues. Pitchers who started ball games very often pitched all nine innings. Today a "complete game," in which a pitcher goes all nine innings, is very rare. Pitchers also used to start games every three or four days, which over the years has become every five days. In the early 1900s pitchers would win 30 games or more in a season, but by the 1930s, and ever since, 20 wins has become the mark to shoot for in a season. Today, only a few pitchers win 20 games in a year.

Pitchers' earned run averages (ERA), telling the average number of runs they allow in a game, have also gone up over the years. Through most of the 1900s, an earned run average under 3.00 per game was excellent, and between 3.00 and 4.00 was very good. Today, only a few pitchers have ERAs under 4.00. In the early and even the mid-1900s, the only time a relief pitcher was called in was if the starting pitcher was doing poorly. Over the past 30 years this has changed, and relief pitchers now come into games much more often. It's not unusual to see three or four pitchers in a game.

The Cy Young Award

The Cy Young Award, named after the pitcher with the most wins in baseball history, is given each year to the best pitcher in each league.

The game has changed over the years, but the basic idea that the pitcher wants to get the batter out remains the same. Below are just a few of the all-time greats. Ask your parents or your grandparents about them; they may have seen them pitch.

Listed below each pitcher are his career wins (W), losses (L), earned run average (ERA), and strikeouts (K). Also listed are the years he played in the majors and the teams on which he spent the majority of his career. Keep in mind that only 20 pitchers have won 300 or more games and only 12 pitchers have 3,000 or more career strikeouts in modern baseball history (since 1903).

Steve Carlton, 1965–1988, Cardinals, Phillies, Giants, White Sox, Indians, Twins

W–L	ERA	K
329–244	3.22	4,176

They just called him "Lefty," because many considered him the greatest left-hander to ever pitch. Carlton came up with St. Louis in 1965, and in 1971 he won 20 games for the first time in his career. Surprisingly, he was then traded to the Phillies, where in 1972 he won 27 games and had an earned run average of 1.97, leading the league. He also had over 300 strikeouts that year and won the coveted Cy Young Award in 1972 as the best pitcher in the National League. He won the award three more times in his long career. By the time Carlton retired he was the ninth all-time pitcher in wins, and he still ranks second all-time in strikeouts. Although he never liked to talk with sportswriters very much, the baseball writers voted him into the Hall of Fame in 1994.

FUN FACT

How Many Cy Young Awards?

The Cy Young Award was first given to Don Newcombe of the Dodgers in 1956. From 1956 through 1966 only one pitcher in the major leagues was given the award. But starting in 1967, one pitcher in each league receives a Cy Young Award.

Carleton's Ks

Steve Carlton once struck out 19 batters in a game, which at the time was a major-league record. Since then, six other pitchers have matched or surpassed that record.

WORDS to KNOW

southpaw: A left-handed pitcher is sometimes referred to as a "southpaw."

Dennis Eckersley, 1975–1998 Red Sox, Indians, Cubs, Athletics, Cardinals

W–L	ERA	K
197–171	3.50	2,401

For many years, relief pitching in major-league baseball meant the starter was doing poorly and the manager would have to go to a "lesser" pitcher who was a reliever. It wasn't until the 1960s that relief pitching became a big part of the game. Eckersley was one of the greatest relievers of the past 30 years, if not the greatest, in a group that included Rollie Fingers, Lee Smith, Sparky Lyle, and several others. Originally a starter and even a 20-game winner in the 1970s, "Eck" became a relief pitcher in 1987 and a full-time closer in 1988. He was amazing! In 1990 his ERA was 0.60. More incredible than that was that in two full seasons combined he walked only seven batters. Between 1988 and 1992 he saved 230 games for the A's, totally baffling opposing hitters. One can only imagine how many saves he could have had if he had been a closer for all of his seemingly endless 23-year career. Eckersley retired in 1998 and was elected to the Hall of Fame in 2004.

Bob Feller, 1936–1956 Indians

W–L	ERA	K
266–162	3.25	2,561

Bob Feller made it to the major leagues in 1936, before his 18th birthday. He grew up on a farm in Iowa and became one of the hardest throwing pitchers of all time, firing fastballs of nearly 100 miles per hour and earning the nickname "Rapid Robert." He led the American League in strikeouts seven times during his career. He won 20 games six times and 266 games in his career. He would have easily won at least 325 had it not been for World War II. Feller did not wait to be drafted into the army. Instead, at age 23 he left an all-star baseball career to serve his country by enlisting in the navy for four years. Feller went from the ballpark to an American battleship. In 1946, he returned to the Indians and to the cheers of the fans, who had waited for him and were very proud of him for serving his country. Feller retired at the age of 38 and made the Hall of Fame in 1962.

WORDS to KNOW

save: When a pitcher comes into a close ball game and gets the final outs, that pitcher earns a save.

WORDS to KNOW

closer: The relief pitcher who comes in to get the final outs is called the team's "closer." Teams didn't usually have closers until the 1970s or 1980s.

WORDS to KNOW

MVP: MVP stands for most valuable player. One player in each league wins the MVP Award every year—not only for being a great player, but usually for helping their team go to the play-offs. The Baseball Writers' Association of America chooses who wins the MVP Award.

Lots of Wins

After winning 416 games as a pitcher, Walter Johnson became a manager and won 530 more games. So he could be said to have won 946 games!

Lefty Grove, 1925–1941 Athletics, Red Sox

W–L	ERA	K
300–141	3.06	2,266

Grove was 25 when he made the majors with the Philadelphia Athletics. By his third season he was a 20-game winner, and in 1931 he went 31–4 while winning the Most Valuable Player Award. In his seven years with the A's, Grove was, in a word, awesome. He led the league in ERA four times, while posting a record of 172 wins and only 41 losses between 1927 and 1933. After a total of nine ERA titles, Grove retired in 1941, ending a 17-year career. During his best years, Grove was as tough a pitcher to hit against as anyone who ever pitched. He won 68 percent of his games and made the Hall of Fame in 1947.

Walter Johnson, 1907–1927 Senators

W–L	ERA	K
416–279	2.16	3,509

Nicknamed "The Big Train," Johnson did everything well: he threw hard, had control, threw a lot of innings, and never seemed to get tired. He came up with the Washington Senators in 1907 at only 19 years of age and began a 21-year career that was truly remarkable. Johnson won 20 or more games per season 10 years in a row, led the league in strikeouts 12 times and in ERA five times, including a 1.14 ERA in 1913 when he won 36 games. His 416 wins are second best of all time; his 110 career shutouts are the most ever. He never won a Cy Young Award since Cy was also still pitching, and the award didn't exist yet. He did, however, win the Most Valuable Player Award on a couple of occasions. Johnson was one of the first five players selected to the Hall of Fame in 1936.

Sandy Koufax, 1955–1966 Dodgers

W–L	ERA	K
165–87	2.76	2,396

Sandy Koufax was born in Brooklyn in 1935 and by the age of 19 was pitching for the hometown favorites, the Brooklyn Dodgers. He was part of the team that picked up in 1957 and moved away to Los Angeles. An average pitcher during his first several seasons, he just got better and better until he led the league in strikeouts in 1961. By 1963, major-league hitters considered him the toughest pitcher in baseball. He posted 25 wins, struck out over 300, and led the league with an ERA of 1.88. He not only won the Cy Young Award as the best pitcher but the Most Valuable Player Award as well. Over the next four years, he won three more Cy Young Awards, leading the league in wins, strikeouts, and ERA each year. He also threw four no-hitters. Unfortunately, Koufax developed serious arthritis in his elbow and by 1967, at the top of his game, was forced to retire. In 1972 he was elected to the Hall of Fame at only 37 years of age. Koufax did not pitch in the major leagues for very long, but he was definitely one of the best in baseball history.

FUN FACT

First MVP Winners

The first-ever winners of the MVP Award were Lefty Grove in the American League, and Frankie Frisch in the National League.

Christy Mathewson, 1900–1916 Giants

W–L	ERA	K
373–188	2.13	2,502

Watching pitchers today struggle to keep an ERA under 4.00, it seems almost impossible to imagine that Christy Mathewson could pitch for 17 years and post a 2.13 career earned run average. Mathewson made the major leagues at the age of 20 in the year 1900. In 1901 he picked up his first of 373 career wins. Back in those days, pitchers threw a lot of innings, and Mathewson topped 300 innings pitched over 11 seasons. Giants manager John McGraw figured, why

WORDS to KNOW

no-hitter: When a pitcher allows no hits in a game, it's called a no-hitter. It's still a no-hitter if the pitcher walks batters, or if batters reach base on fielding errors. In fact, it's possible for a pitcher to pitch a no-hitter but still lose the game!

FUN FACT

Thirty-Game Winner

The last pitcher to top the 30-win mark was Denny McLain, who won 31 games for the Detroit Tigers in 1968. He's the only pitcher to win more than 30 games in a season in over 60 years!

not let him pitch a lot, he was almost impossible to score on. Mathewson rattled off a string of 12 consecutive seasons of 20 or more wins, with a high of 37 in 1908. He was the National League's best pitcher for the first decade of the 20th century. In 1939 he was one of the first five players ever to be elected to the Hall of Fame with Ruth, Cobb, Wagner, and Johnson.

Satchel Paige, 1926–1953 Black Lookouts, Black Barons, Black Sox, American Giants, Colored Giants, Monarchs, Indians, Browns

W–L	ERA	K
28–31	3.29	288

[major-league totals only]

Satchel Paige may well have been the primary player responsible for racial integration of the major leagues. He played for a variety of Negro League teams from 1926 to 1947, moving from team to team depending on who could pay him the most money. Americans, black or white, were willing to pay to see Paige pitch. His reputation as one of the greatest pitchers in baseball was well established before World War II, during which he raised money for the war effort through his pitching exhibitions. He played with Negro League all-stars in competitive exhibition games against major leaguers. Finally, after Jackie Robinson broke in with the Dodgers, Paige was signed to a major-league contract with the Cleveland Indians in 1948 at age 42. He played two seasons with the Indians, then moved with owner Bill Veeck to the St. Louis Browns, where he made the all-star team. His career totals look poor compared to the other pitchers in this list; but bear in mind, Paige put up these numbers over only five seasons, and he was 47 years old during that last season. One can only imagine the kind of career stats Paige could have earned had he played all of those 27 years in the major leagues.

Nolan Ryan, 1966–1993 Mets, Angels, Astros, Rangers

W–L	ERA	K
324–292	3.19	5,386

There are few athletes that can match the accomplishments of Nolan Ryan. He was truly a flame-thrower, firing the ball harder and faster than anyone had ever seen. When Ryan came up with the Mets in 1966 he could throw very hard, but he had control problems and walked a lot of hitters. In 1972 the Mets traded him to the California Angels, and there he turned into a big winner and became the king of strikeouts. He led the league 11 times in strikeouts, once having as many as 383 in a season. While most pitchers would be thrilled to throw one no-hitter in their careers, Ryan set a major league record by throwing seven. That's right, seven! A native of Texas, Ryan was excited when he got to play for the Houston Astros, where he topped Walter Johnson's long-held all-time career strikeout record in 1983 at the age of 36. Ryan, however, was far from done. Somehow, no matter how hard he threw, his arm never seemed to get tired. He surprised everyone by pitching in the big leagues for another 10 years until he finally retired at age 46. By that time he had over 5,000 strikeouts, far more than anyone else. He made the Hall of Fame in 1999.

The Ryan Express

"You can't hit what you can't see" was the familiar complaint of batters who struck out time and again trying to hit a Nolan Ryan fastball, which became known as "The Ryan Express."

Tom Seaver, 1967–1986 Mets, Reds, White Sox, Red Sox

W–L	ERA	K
311–205	2.86	3,640

WORDS to KNOW

perfect game: When a pitcher does not allow anyone to reach base at all, it's called a perfect game. Only 17 pitchers have ever pitched a perfect game.

When "Tom Terrific" came up with the New York Mets in 1967, the Mets were the worst team in the major leagues. By 1969, they shocked everyone and won 100 games, with Tom Seaver winning 25 of them on the way to a World Championship. Seaver won his first of three Cy Young Awards that year and became the heart and soul of the Mets. In 1973 he led the Mets back to the World Series, but this time they lost to the A's. When he was traded away in 1977 Mets fans were very upset, but Reds fans were excited. After some successful years in Cincinnati, he returned to the Mets for a short time in 1983, but it was near the end of his long career. Tom won 20 or more games four times and led the league in strikeouts five times. Seaver retired as one of the 20 winningest pitchers of all time, and he sits fourth all-time in strikeouts. He was elected to the Hall of Fame in 1992 and even after that returned to the Mets one more time, only this time as an announcer in their broadcasting booth.

Cy Young 1890–1911 Spiders, Cardinals, Perfectos, Browns, Red Sox, Americans, Somersets, Pilgrims, Naps, Indians, Braves

W–L	ERA	K
511–315	2.63	2,800

Cy Young, nicknamed "Cyclone" because of how hard he threw, was born in 1867. His career spanned from 1890 to 1911. His 511 wins and 7,377 innings pitched are by far the most ever, and it's hard to believe that any modern pitcher could top these records. Young threw three no-hitters during his career and once pitched 44 consecutive scoreless innings. To give you an idea of how much he pitched, consider that today the best pitchers throw maybe six or seven complete games in a season—and Cy Young completed nearly 750 games, or almost 34 per season. Needless to say, he was elected into the Hall of Fame in 1937. He died in 1955, and in 1956, in his honor, the Cy Young Award was established for the best pitcher each year in baseball.

Hitters

The basic idea of hitting hasn't changed all that much over the years. The type of hits changed in the 1920s from mostly singles and doubles to plenty of home runs, thanks to Babe Ruth. Even with more home runs, the best major-league ballplayers aimed for a batting average of over .300. In the early part of the 20th century some hitters topped .400, but fielders wore smaller gloves, which may have been part of the reason for such high averages. No one has hit over .400 in the major leagues since Ted Williams in 1941. In the late 1960s there were fewer .300 hitters, and pitchers dominated the game. By the 1990s, however, home runs were flying out of ballparks at an amazing rate, and there were plenty of hitters batting well into the high .300s.

Over the years there have been many great hitters, but only a few managed to hit, run, and field at the highest level for many years. Many of the superstars featured here not only hit for power but stole bases, and most importantly, they were the guys you could count on when you needed the big hit to win a game. These are just a few of the game's biggest superstars and most popular all-time favorites.

Under each hitter is his career home run total (HR), runs batted in total (RBI), and batting average (AVG). Only 16 players have topped 500 home runs, while 1,500 runs batted in, 3,000 hits, and a career average over .300 are all benchmark totals of the best players in the game.

FUN FACT

Shhh!

Perhaps Cy Young wouldn't want to mention it, but besides the most wins ever, he also holds the record for the most losses ever at 315. Of course, that's because he played more games than any other pitcher!

A Baseball Coincidence

Odd as it may seem, in *The Baseball Encyclopedia*, which has over 1,000 pages of players listed, the first player in the book (alphabetically) is also the player with the most home runs, Hank Aaron.

Henry (Hank) Aaron 1954–1976 Braves, Brewers

HR	RBI	AVG
755	2,297	.305

Many people thought Babe Ruth's record of 714 career home runs might never be broken. Hank Aaron, nicknamed "The Hammer," had another idea. Aaron played briefly in the Negro Leagues before being signed in 1954 by the Milwaukee Braves, who moved to Atlanta in 1966.

Aaron never topped fifty homers in a season, but belted at least 25 home runs 18 times, with a high of 47. He also posted over 120 RBIs seven times while setting the all-time career RBI record. By the time he finished his 23-year career, back in Milwaukee as a member of the Brewers, he was also near the top in games played, hits, runs scored, and doubles. Aaron made the Hall of Fame in 1982.

Johnny Bench, 1967–1983 Reds

HR	RBI	AVG
389	1,376	.267

There was never a greater major-league catcher than Johnny Bench. He broke into the major leagues in style at 20 years old, making the All-Star game and winning Rookie of the Year honors. In 1970, his third season, Bench won the National League MVP with 45 homers and 148 RBIs while leading the Reds to the World Series. Bench topped the 100 RBI mark on five occasions as the main cog in Cincinnati's "Big Red Machine," the nickname for the Reds' great team of the '70s.

Besides his tremendous power hitting and many clutch hits, Bench was also an incredible defensive catcher with a

FUN FACT

Brothers Who Hit Home Runs

There have been many brothers who played major-league baseball, from Joe and Dom DiMaggio to Cal and Billy Ripken to Aaron and Bret Boone. But who were the brothers who hit the most combined home runs? Hank and Tommy Aaron. Hammerin' Hank hit 755, while Tommie added on just 13 for a total of 768.

great throwing arm. He won 10 Gold Glove Awards as the best defensive catcher in the National League until injuries forced him to spend more time at third and first base. Two World Championships and his consistent play made Johnny Bench a household name as one of baseball's most popular players of the 1970s. The injuries from catching, however, caught up with him, and by age 35 Bench had to call it quits. In 1989 he was elected to the Hall of Fame.

A Baseball Coincidence

Roger Maris broke Babe Ruth's single-season home run record, hitting 61 homers, in 1961.

Roberto Clemente, 1955–1972 Pirates

HR	RBI	AVG
240	1,305	.317

Clemente was a tremendous all-around ballplayer. He not only could hit for a high average, but he had power and was a super defensive outfielder, winning 12 Gold Gloves. He joined the Pirates in the mid-1950s as a 20-year-old rookie from Puerto Rico. He went on to become the greatest player from Puerto Rico and the first Hispanic player elected to the Hall of Fame. Four times in the 1960s Clemente led the National League in batting, and four times he had over 200 hits in a season. He appeared in two World Series for the Pirates and batted .362 overall, helping lead the Pirates to the title in 1971. Clemente became one of the few players to get his 3,000th hit, which came at the end of the 1972 season. It would be his last hit ever. On New Year's Eve of that year he was on his way to deliver supplies to victims of a severe earthquake in Nicaragua when the plane he was on crashed. Clemente died at age 38 but is remembered as a hero both on and off the field.

Play Ball

A baseball player must be sure to follow the rules of the game, or he could get sent to the dugout! You must carefully follow the directions below to learn the word that finishes the following popular saying: "Some people say that playing baseball is as American as eating _____."

1. Print the word BASEBALL.   BASEBALL

2. Switch the position of the first two letters.

3. Move the 5th letter between the 2nd and 3rd letters.

4. Switch the positions of the 4th and 8th letters.

5. Change the 6th letter to P.

6. Change the last letter to E.

7. Change both B s to P s.

8. Change the 7th letter to I.

Ty Cobb, 1905–1928 Tigers, Athletics

HR	RBI	AVG
118	1,961	.357

Cobb was one of the toughest players of all time. He worked very hard and spent hours practicing hitting, sliding, and throwing while on his way to the major leagues in 1905 at the age of 18. The hard work paid off. Cobb played 24 years, almost all for the Tigers, and hit under .300 just once, as a rookie. In fact, he batted over .400 three times and led the league in batting average 12 times on his way to an incredible all-time high .357 career batting average. Not only was he a great hitter, but Cobb was one of the best base stealers ever, stealing nearly 900 bases. Cobb's great hitting made him one of the first five players elected to the Hall of Fame. The fans enjoyed watching Cobb play, but he rarely got along with his teammates, and opposing players hated him. He would sharpen his spikes before the game and then slide in hard, feet first. Cobb said when he was older that if he had one thing he could do differently it would be to have more friends.

Joe DiMaggio, 1936–1951 Yankees

HR	RBI	AVG
361	1,537	.325

"Joltin' Joe" and "The Yankee Clipper" were two nicknames for the great Yankee center fielder of the 1930s and '40s. He was as popular and well liked on and off the field as any baseball player ever. The most valuable player in 1941, DiMaggio not only hit .351 while driving in 125 runs, but he only struck out 13 times! DiMaggio's marvelous career was highlighted by his amazing streak of getting a hit in 56 consecutive games. No one has come within a dozen games of matching that mark set in 1941. Three years spent in the

WORDS to KNOW

player-manager: Occasionally the manager of a team is also a player, referred to as the player-manager. Hiring a player to manage the team was more typical of teams from long ago. The only player-manager in the last few decades was Pete Rose, who played for and managed the Reds in 1985 and 1986.

Manager, Too

Cobb not only played for the Tigers, but for six years was a player-manager for them, too, amassing a 479–444 record. He took the Tigers as high as second place in the American League.

army and injuries limited DiMaggio to only 13 years in the big leagues, but he helped lead the Yankees to the World Series 10 times in those 13 seasons. He was elected to the Hall of Fame in 1955. DiMaggio remained famous for many years after playing baseball. He married legendary movie actress Marilyn Monroe, owned a popular restaurant in San Francisco, did many TV commercials, was mentioned in the novel *The Old Man and the Sea*, and in the hit song "Mrs. Robinson." "Joltin' Joe" certainly was a legend.

Jimmie Foxx, 1925–1945 Athletics, Red Sox

HR	RBI	AVG
534	1,922	.325

The "Double X" they called him, and he was one of the most feared hitters of the 1920s and '30s. Playing in the shadow of "The Babe" and Lou Gehrig, Foxx slugged over 30 homers a year for 12 consecutive seasons, hitting 58 in 1932 while winning the Triple Crown. He also topped the 100 RBI mark 13 straight years, with totals as high as 169 and 175. Even though Foxx led the A's to three pennants, manager Connie Mack didn't want to pay him more money in 1935. In fact, he tried to cut Foxx's salary. Foxx would not play for less money and was sent to the Red Sox where he continued to clobber American League pitching before playing briefly for the Cubs and Phillies at the end of his 20-year career. Foxx was a dominant hitter and one of the biggest stars of the '20s and '30s, respected by everyone in baseball. He was elected to the Hall of Fame in 1951.

Lou Gehrig, 1923–1939 Yankees

HR	RBI	AVG
493	1,995	.340

He was called the Iron Horse because he was always in the lineup. Gehrig batted right after "The Babe" in the great Yankees lineup and played in the shadow of Ruth, who was more charismatic than the quiet Gehrig. Nonetheless, Gehrig was as awesome a hitter as anyone. For 14 consecutive years he drove in over 100 runs, topping 170 three times, including an American League record 184 in 1931. He could do it all, getting over 200 hits eight times, 40 home runs five times, and batting over .300 for 13 consecutive years. His 23 grand slam home runs is the all-time high.

Despite all of his amazing accomplishments, Gehrig is best known for two things. He began a streak in 1925 where he played every single game until 1939, or 2,130 consecutive games, a record most people thought would never be broken. Cal Ripken Jr. has since topped that incredible record. Unfortunately, the other thing Gehrig is best remembered for is the reason that eight games into the 1939 season he removed himself from the lineup. Gehrig had been suffering from an unknown disease, later called Lou Gehrig's disease. He retired from baseball in May of 1939, and in July he described himself as the "luckiest man on earth" for the opportunity to have played for the Yankees, and to have been loved by the fans and by his wife. Less than two years later he died at the age of 37. He was elected into the Hall of Fame in 1939.

> **Pride of the Yankees, Gehrig's Story**
>
> The movie *The Pride of the Yankees* is a marvelous, deeply touching story of this great, courageous man.

Tony Gwynn, 1982–2001 Padres

HR	RBI	AVG
135	1,138	.338

From the moment he came up to the big leagues, Gwynn was the best hitter in baseball and one of the best of all time. His career .338 average is up there with the greats of the early 1900s, and in 1994 he came within 6 points of batting .400, something that hadn't been done since 1941. Gwynn led the league in batting seven times, hitting over .360 four times. He could hit any pitch for a single or double and hardly ever struck out, which helps explain why he had over 3,000 career hits. In his younger years he was also a great base stealer and tremendous defensive player. Gwynn retired at the end of the 2001 season after 20 years with the San Diego Padres and 19 consecutive .300 seasons. Gwynn was inducted into the Hall of Fame in 2007.

Rogers Hornsby, 1915–1937 Cardinals, Giants, Red Sox, Cubs, Browns

HR	RBI	AVG
301	1,584	.358

He was called by those who saw him play and many baseball historians the greatest right-handed hitter in baseball history (Babe Ruth hit from the left side). A dedicated hitter, Hornsby believed that watching movies, drinking coffee, and drinking alcohol would affect his eye at the plate, so he avoided all of those habits. Starting in 1921 he posted a combined five-year average of .402, which was, in a word, amazing. But Hornsby wasn't just hitting singles on his way to a .358 career average—second all-time to Cobb. He led the league several times in doubles and home runs and posted over 10 triples in a season nine times. Twice Hornsby won the Triple Crown, and twice he won the MVP. He went on to

FUN FACT

Your Batting Coach Can Be Useful

Rogers Hornsby was such a great hitter that at the age of 66 he was hired as the New York Mets' batting coach. The Mets lost 120 games that year—apparently they didn't listen to him.

be a player-manager in 1926 and was very successful. The problem was, as good a hitter and manager as Hornsby was, he was very demanding, unfriendly, and considered downright mean. In the late 1920s he was traded from team to team since he wasn't well liked around the clubhouse. Hornsby made the Hall of Fame in 1942.

Reggie Jackson, 1967–1987 A's, Orioles, Yankees, Angels

HR	RBI	AVG
563	1,702	.262

"Mr. October" was Reggie's nickname, because when it was World Series time (in October), he was awesome. A great power hitter even in his rookie year in 1967, Jackson went on to lead the league in home runs four times during his career and end up sixth on the all-time list when he retired. Jackson helped the Oakland A's win three consecutive World Series championships in 1972, '73, and '74. He later joined the Yankees and helped lead them to the World Series three times and to win two more World Championships. Reggie struck out a lot and wasn't a great defensive star, but when it was an important game, he was at his best. In Game 6 of the 1977 World Series, Jackson had what many consider the single best World Series game of any hitter ever. He hit three tremendous home runs and drove in five runs in the game. Jackson was outspoken and very popular everywhere he went through his entire career. He made the Hall of Fame in 1993.

Switch Hitters

Some hitters bat from the right side and some from the left, but if you can hit from both sides of the plate, you're called a switch hitter. The greatest switch hitter of all time was Mickey Mantle. He holds the record for hitting home runs in the same game from both sides of the plate nine different times.

Mickey Mantle, 1951–1968 Yankees

HR	RBI	AVG
536	1,509	.298

When Joe DiMaggio retired in 1951, someone had to fill his shoes, and that was a tall order because he was one of the greatest ever. Sure enough, the Yankees found another superstar, from the town of Spavinaw, Oklahoma: "The Mick," as he was called. Mantle was a star in all aspects of the game. He hit for power, for average, in the clutch, and for a while he even stole bases. Starting in 1953 Mantle rattled off nine straight 100+ RBI seasons. He led the league in homers with 52 in 1956 while winning the Triple Crown and MVP. His 54 homers in 1961 would have led most seasons, but teammate Roger Maris showed him up by hitting a record 61. Unfortunately, by 1965 injuries made it difficult for Mantle to play at the same level he had for so many years. Bad knees caused Mantle to move to first base, where he played until 1968. For a span of 12 out of 14 years between 1951 and 1964 the Yankees went to the World Series, largely because of Mantle. His 18 home runs and 40 RBIs in 65 World Series games are all-time records. Mantle was popular on and off the field, a Yankee legend powering the team to pennant after pennant. He made the Hall of Fame in 1974.

Willie Mays, 1951–1973 Giants, Mets

HR	RBI	AVG
660	1,903	.302

They called him the "Say Hey Kid," and he was one of the greatest and most likable players to ever play the game. After his rookie season in 1951, Mays spent two years in the army before returning to the (then New York) Giants and leading them with 41 homers to the World Championship over the Cleveland Indians. Willie could do it all. He hit for power, leading the league in homers four times, and he also had great speed, leading the league in stolen bases four times. He was known for incredible defense, with his basket catch, using the glove as a "basket" and catching fly balls at his waist. Perhaps the most famous catch ever made by Mays came in the first game of the 1954 World Series as he grabbed a ball going over his head in the deepest part of center field to help the Giants hold on and win. After many years with the Giants in San Francisco, Mays spent his last couple of years back in New York with the Mets before retiring as the third-greatest home run hitter ever. A baseball legend, Mays made the Hall of Fame in 1979.

Stan Musial, 1941–1963 Cardinals

HR	RBI	AVG
475	1,951	.331

One of the most feared hitters in the 1940s and '50s was Stan "The Man" Musial. He started as a pitcher in the minor leagues, but an arm injury forced him to switch to playing the outfield. At 23 years old in his second season he won the MVP, which was the first of four he collected in his 21 incredible seasons. Stan could hit for power, drive in runs, and hit for a high average, leading the league in batting seven times. He worked very hard perfecting his swing, and many young players wanted to learn from him. He spent his entire career with one team, the St. Louis Cardinals, and holds most of the Cardinals' all-time hitting records. Musial was elected to the Hall of Fame in 1969.

About Willie Mays

Former Dodger player and manager Gil Hodges talked about how good a defensive player Willie Mays really was. "I can't very well tell my hitters, don't hit it to him. Wherever they hit it, he's always there."

Classic Game

For over 40 years, Strat-O-Matic has been making the ideal baseball board game. Complete with year-by-year stats for each major league player, the game is fun for fans of all ages. You can select your favorite team from the past season, or pick up some classic teams from years gone by. There is a computerized version, but the standard version with cards and dice is still as wonderful as ever. Look at *www.strat-o-matic.com* to find out more.

Cal Ripken Jr., 1981–2001 Orioles

HR	RBI	AVG
431	1,695	.276

Ripken was named Rookie of the Year in 1982, the MVP in 1983 and again in 1991, and established himself as one of the top players in recent baseball. One thing that could be said for Ripken was that he always came to play, and play hard, day in and day out. In late 1995, he went from a star to a legend as he broke a record that most thought could never be topped. Ripken played in his 2,131st consecutive game, breaking the iron horse record set by the late great Lou Gehrig. Ripken played another 501 more consecutive games before taking himself out of the lineup in September of 1998. During the 2001 season, Ripken announced his retirement after 20 years with the Orioles. He was inducted into the Hall of Fame in 2007. In his career, Ripken played in 3,001 games, had 3,184 hits, 431 home runs, and nearly 1,700 RBIs. He was also one of the best liked and most respected individuals who ever played in the major leagues.

Frank Robinson, 1956–1976 Reds, Orioles, Dodgers, Angels, Indians

HR	RBI	AVG
586	1,812	.294

From his Rookie of the Year season in 1956, the Texas-born Robinson made it obvious that he was going to be a star. In the shadow of Mays, Mantle, and Aaron, Robinson very quietly hit over 30 home runs season after season while consistently batting over .300. The Reds, however, felt they could do better, so after the 1965 season they traded Robinson to the Orioles for two pitchers and an outfielder. He responded to being traded by hitting 49 home runs, driving in 122 runs, and batting .316, winning the Triple Crown, the MVP, and leading the Orioles to a sweep over the Dodgers in the World Series—he was also World Series MVP that year. The Reds regretted trading him. He later topped the 500 home run mark while with the Orioles before playing for several other teams near the end of his 21-year career. When he retired he was fourth all-time in home runs. Robinson also became the major leagues' first black manager in 1975, while still playing for the Cleveland Indians. He was elected to the Hall of Fame in 1982.

Jackie Robinson, 1947–1956 Dodgers

HR	RBI	AVG
137	734	.311

Jackie Robinson broke into the major leagues with the Brooklyn Dodgers in 1947 at the age of 28 after several years in the Negro Leagues. He led the league in stolen bases and won Rookie of the Year honors. But his entry into the majors was far more significant than his stats. Robinson broke the "color barrier," becoming the first black player to play in the major leagues, at least since the late 1800s. Making a major statement for his race wasn't new to Robinson, who had been court-martialed out of the United States Army after he had refused to sit in the back of a bus because of the color of his skin.

The early days of his career were very difficult. Fans, players on other teams, and even many of his own teammates were cruel. Some players even started a petition that said they would not play in the game with him. Somehow, he put up with all the torment and continued proving himself as a first-rate ballplayer.

In 1949 Robinson hit .342, which led the league in batting, and he was named the MVP. In the span of just 10 years he would make a huge breakthrough for the game of baseball. Robinson's legacy continued long after his seven

FUN FACT

Two-Time MVP Winners

Ten players have won the National League MVP Award more than once. By coincidence, there is one at each position, so you could field an all-MVP team: pitcher Carl Hubbell, catchers Johnny Bench and Roy Campanella, first baseman Stan Musial (even though he started as an outfielder), second baseman Joe Morgan, shortstop Ernie Banks, third baseman Mike Schmidt, and outfielders Willie Mays, Dale Murphy, and Barry Bonds. Quite a team, huh?

World Series appearances or his induction into the Hall of Fame in 1962. In 1997 at stadiums all over the country, the 50-year anniversary of Robinson's achievement was honored. His uniform number, 42, was retired throughout major-league baseball. Though Jackie Robinson will be remembered foremost for breaking baseball's color barrier, it must be noted that his performance earned him recognition as one of the all-time greatest players of any color.

Switch Hitter

Can you see the 10 differences between the two pictures of this batter?

HINT: It doesn't count that he's facing in different directions—that's what a switch hitter does!

Who's Who?

Some baseball nicknames are easy to guess. For example, almost all players who have had the last name "Rhodes" have gotten the nickname "Dusty." See how many of the famous nicknames on the left you can match with the real names on the right. Put the number of the correct nickname on the line in front of each real name.

HINT: For those names you can't figure out, or don't know already, look through this book. They're in here somewhere!

1. The Big Train
2. Tom Terrific
3. Cyclone
4. Joltin' Joe
5. Double X
6. Mr. October
7. The Mick
8. Say Hey Kid
9. Stan The Man
10. Charlie Hustle
11. Wizard of Oz
12. The Big Unit
13. The Rocket

___ Cy Young
___ Jimmy Foxx
___ Joe DiMaggio
___ Mickey Mantle
___ Ozzie Smith
___ Pete Rose
___ Randy Johnson
___ Reggie Jackson
___ Roger Clemens
___ Stan Musial
___ Tom Seaver
___ Walter Johnson
___ Willie Mays

Look! It's "Bubbles" MacCoy!

Home Run Rate

Babe Ruth hit home runs at an incredible rate, averaging 43 per season over a span of 16 years, in an era where even 20 to 30 home runs in a season was considered outstanding.

Boo!

Philadelphia is known as a tough town in which to be a sports star. The fans take pride in yelling "Boo!" all the time. In fact, even though Phillies fans worship Mike Schmidt as one of their town's best professional athletes ever, the Veteran's Stadium crowd once booed Mike Schmidt. But that shouldn't make him feel too bad— Philadelphia fans famously booed Santa Claus at a football game!

Pete Rose, 1963–1986 Reds, Phillies, Expos

HR	RBI	AVG
160	1,314	.303

They called him "Charlie Hustle" because he ran out every play, even when he drew a walk. No one played the game harder than Pete Rose. He was one of the most intense players of his time, in a career that spanned 24 years. He played outfield, third base, second base, and first base before becoming a player-manager. Rose had grown up in Cincinnati, so the Reds were his hometown team, and he became their hero as part of the Big Red Machine of the 1970s. Eight times he had more than 200 hits in a season on his way to becoming the all-time leader in base hits. Rose was a tremendous singles and doubles hitter who led the league in batting three times, but more than anything he was a tireless player. By the time he retired he not only had more hits but more at-bats and had played in more games than anyone else.

After his career ended it was found that Rose had bet on baseball games while manager of the Reds. The evidence pointed toward Rose's involvement with gamblers, and Rose has since admitted the truth of these charges. He was suspended from professional baseball activities for life; thus, he is not eligible for election to the Hall of Fame.

Babe Ruth, 1914–1935 Red Sox, Yankees, Braves

HR	RBI	AVG	W–L	ERA	K
714	2,213	.342	94–46	2.28	488

It's almost impossible to find anyone who hasn't heard of "The Babe." "The Bambino," as he was also nicknamed, George Herman "Babe" Ruth could do it all. He began as a pitcher with the Boston Red Sox (and a good one) before moving to the outfield. He went on to change the face of baseball. When Ruth led the major leagues with 29 home runs in 1919 it was the first time a player had hit more than 25 in a season. He was traded to the Yankees, where he became the greatest home run hitter ever. His 714 home runs stood as the record until Hank Aaron passed that mark in 1974. Had Ruth not been a pitcher for several years, who knows how many he would have hit. He led the league in home runs (or tied for the lead) twelve times. He also batted .342 for his career and is still considered by most baseball historians as the greatest baseball player ever. Ruth led the Yankees to one World Series title after another. An often-told story says that in one World Series against the Cubs, Ruth stepped up to the plate, pointed to the bleachers where he was going to hit a home run . . . and then did just that.

Beyond baseball, Ruth was an enormously popular celebrity and was treated like royalty. The Babe enjoyed all the publicity and excitement that surrounded him. It was said that "as he moved, center stage moved with him." Ruth retired in 1935 and was one of the first five players elected to the Hall of Fame in 1939. Yankee stadium is still called the House That Ruth Built.

WORDS to KNOW

Gold Glove Award: Each year the best fielder at each position in both the National and American leagues is given the Gold Glove Award for fielding excellence.

Mike Schmidt, 1972–1989 Phillies

HR	RBI	AVG
548	1,595	.267

Mike Schmidt is considered by many to be the best all-around third baseman ever to play the game. He was a truly awesome power hitter, leading the league eight times in home runs. In just 17 years he placed himself in the top 10 all-time in homers, won three MVPs, and helped lead the Phillies to their only World Championship. On the other side of the field, he was a tremendous defensive player. He won the Gold Glove as the best fielding third baseman in the National League nine times. He went about his business very seriously and the fans of the Philadelphia Phillies, as well as other players, respected and admired his talent and his work ethic. Schmidt retired in 1989 and was elected to the Hall of Fame in 1995.

Ozzie Smith, 1978–1996 Padres, Cardinals

HR	RBI	AVG
28	793	.262

How can a player with those kind of career numbers be included in this list of the all-time greats, you may wonder? Just 28 homers in 19 years? Smith represents the other side of the game: defense. They called him the "Wizard of Oz" because no one had ever played shortstop like Ozzie. He could get to groundballs that no one else could reach, often diving in either direction. He would then somehow make the throw to first base for the out. He could also turn double plays like nobody else, turning more than any player in history. He dazzled the fans and frustrated the opponents who thought they had a hit until somehow Ozzie turned it into an out. He won a record 13 Gold Gloves and led the league nine times in fielding percentage at shortstop. When Ozzie

A Baseball Coincidence

In 1963 the National League home run leaders were number 44 on the Giants, Willie McCovey, and number 44 on the Braves, Hank Aaron. Guess how many they each hit—44!

came up he wasn't much of a hitter, but by the late 1980s he had established himself as a decent batter who drew plenty of walks. He could also steal bases, picking up 580 in his 19-year career, or over 30 per year. Smith was a team leader and a fan favorite. He retired in 1996 and joined the Hall of Fame in 2002.

Honus Wagner, 1897–1917 Pirates

HR	RBI	AVG
101	1,698	.329

Wagner was one of the first superstars of baseball. He began his career just before the 1900s and was a terrific hitter, base stealer, and a flawless fielder. For 17 years he batted over .300 and led the National League eight times in batting average. He also led the league six times in stolen bases and had over 700 in his career. Playing for the Pirates, Wagner was the shortstop in the first World Series ever played in 1903. In 1909 Wagner asked that the tobacco company printing his baseball card stop making them because he felt that smoking set a bad example for children. Only a few of the cards remained, and today a 1909 Honus Wagner card is the most expensive baseball card you could find, worth more than half a million dollars. Many baseball historians still consider Wagner the greatest all-around shortstop ever, and he was one of a few at that position on the All-Century Team. Wagner was also one of the first five players to go into the Hall of Fame in 1939.

Ted Williams, 1939–1960 Red Sox

HR	RBI	AVG
521	1,839	.344

Ted Williams, known as "The Splendid Splinter," was one of the most remarkable hitters ever. He hit for power, for a high average, and rarely ever struck out. In fact, after his career he wrote a book called *The Science of Hitting*, which is still a terrific book to read for anyone who wants to learn to be a better hitter. As a rookie in 1939, Williams hit .327 and a couple of years later batted .406. Well over half a century later, no one has batted over .400 for a season since. The following year in 1942, he not only led the league in batting average again, but also led with 37 home runs and 137 runs batted in, winning the Triple Crown. Williams's career was interrupted twice, once when he was drafted into the navy for World War II, and the other time when he volunteered to serve in the Korean War. Both times he returned to baseball to have great seasons. Williams finally called it quits at age 42 and was inducted into the Hall of Fame in 1965.

Baseball Hangman

Sitting in a restaurant waiting for the waiter to bring your food? If you've got a pen and a paper placemat you can play baseball hangman, featuring major-league players current, past, or on your favorite team. Choose your category depending on how well you and your opponent know baseball. Put down blank spaces for the letters in the player's name, such as _ _ _ _ _ _ _ _ _. Then guess letters as in the game hangman, and draw a *hangman* rope and stick figure. For each wrong guess, have your opponent guess the name before he or she is hanged.

Chapter 4
Great Players of Today

There are a lot of fabulous ballplayers in the major leagues today. A few will end up in the Hall of Fame, while others will simply be remembered for a few magical moments. One of the great things about baseball is that on any given day anyone can be the big hero. The ones you'll read about in this chapter, however, are players who have been big heroes on a consistent basis. These are today's stars who could be tomorrow's Hall-of-Famers.

Premier Pitchers

At a time when home runs are flying out of the ballparks, there are still a few pitchers that shine above and beyond the rest. These first two have been great for a long, long time:

Pedro Martinez

Pedro's older brother spent years as an ace pitcher for the Dodgers, so when Pedro came up (also with the Dodgers) a lot was expected of him. He didn't disappoint. In his first full season he pitched mostly in relief and struck out 119 batters in only 107 innings. He was traded to Montreal, where he became one of the top pitchers in the league. In 1997 he posted a 1.90 ERA and struck out 305 batters, winning the NL Cy Young Award. But it was in Boston where Pedro took his pitching to an even higher level. His first two seasons with the Red Sox produced 42 wins, 11 losses, and an American League Cy Young Award. He led the Sox to the 2004 World Series Title. In 2005 he signed with the Mets, and has been dominating the National League.

Baseball on TV

Baseball has figured in the plot or back-story of lots of television shows. On *Cheers,* Sam used to be a pitcher for the Boston Red Sox. On *Seinfeld,* George works for Yankees owner George Steinbrenner. But perhaps the most famous baseball TV show ever was the episode of *The Simpsons* in which nine major-league players decided to play for Mr. Burns's power plant softball team alongside Homer.

Famous Fungo!

Can you match the silly answers to the funny riddles?

1. What do you call a baseball player who only hits flap-jacks?

2. What do you call a baseball player who throws dairy products?

3. What do you call a dog that stands behind home plate?

_____ A milk pitcher!

_____ A catcher's mutt!

_____ A pancake batter!

A "fungo" is actually a ball hit to the infield during fielding practice. Fungoes are hit with a special thin, light bat called a "fungo stick"!

John Smoltz

Smoltz came up in 1988 with the Braves, and has been an integral part of their National League dominance. He, Greg Maddux, and Tom Glavine were the anchors of the Braves starting rotation for over a decade. Smoltz was the Braves' best postseason pitcher, amassing a record of 14–4 with a 2.70 ERA in the playoffs and World Series. In 2001, an elbow injury forced Smoltz to try his hand at relief pitching, a role at which he excelled. Smoltz earned 154 saves in just over three seasons as the Atlanta closer. Maddux and Glavine have moved on to other teams, but Smoltz has remained with Atlanta. In 2005 he returned to the starting rotation, and his stuff was every bit as good as it was before the elbow injury.

Mariano Rivera

Rivera pitched in his 13th season with the Yankees in 2007. He has been the rock of the Yankees bullpen though their recent years of dominance. Rivera has pitched in the postseason in every year of his career, compiling an incredible postseason ERA of 0.80. Think about it—in the postseason, he was pitching only against the best teams in the American and National leagues. He has pitched 112 postseason innings, which is much more than a full regular season's worth of relief work. And in those 112 innings, he has allowed—get this—only 10 earned runs. Some pitchers give that up in two games!

Trevor Hoffman

Hoffman of the Padres has been a solid closer for a long time. He's recorded more than 30 saves every year since 1995—except for 2003, when he was injured. Since that injury, his performance has been, if possible, even more spectacular. Padres opponents know that if they aren't ahead in the eighth inning, Hoffman is likely to shut the game down.

Top Hitters

A great hitter produces big-time statistics . . . but the best hitters are also those players who thrive in clutch situations. Pitchers certainly do *not* want to face any of these guys with the game on the line.

Ichiro Suzuki

Suzuki was the first nonpitcher from the Japanese professional leagues to sign with a major-league team. He came to the Seattle Mariners in 2001, after he played for nine years for the Orix Blue Wave in Japan. Suzuki does not hit a lot of home runs; yet he might be the best hitter in the game. He established the record for the most hits in a season, with 262, and has more than 200 hits in each of his major-league seasons. He has stolen more than 30 bases in all of his major-league seasons. In 2004, he led the American League with an average of .372, a Mariners record. On defense, Suzuki's strong arm keeps runners from advancing. Ichiro is not a flashy player, but is perhaps the best and most consistent all-around player in the game today.

Albert Pujols

The Cardinals' first baseman has only been in the majors since 2001, but he has established himself as a hitter to be feared. He can hit for power and for average; he rarely strikes out. In fact, he has walked more times than he has struck out. In 2003 Pujols became the youngest player ever to win a batting title. In 2004, he led the Cardinals to the World Series. In 2006, he led them to the World Championship. And still, Pujols continues to work hard to improve his game. He is quite proud of his improved defense at first base.

Derek Jeter

The Yankees' shortstop is also their captain, the undisputed leader of a team that has made the postseason every year since 1995. The highlight of his career must be his game-winning home run in extra innings at Yankee

Stadium in Game 4 of the 2001 World Series. But the highlights that define Jeter's play are his defensive gems. Opposing teams get sick of seeing video clips of Jeter picking up a ground ball deep in the hole, throwing off balance, and robbing the batter of a hit. In an AL division series against the Oakland A's, Jeter came out of nowhere to catch an errant throw from an outfielder, nailing an Oakland runner at home and saving the series for the Yankees. In a 2004 game against the archrival Red Sox, he dived into the stands to catch a foul pop in extra innings, lacerating his chin but helping out an eventual Yankees win. Jeter is one of New York City's most adored celebrities in addition to being the Yankees' most consistent player.

Alex Rodriguez

Through 11 seasons, A-Rod has already hit 401 home runs, including a career high 57 for Texas in 2002. He consistently scores over 100 runs, drives in over 100 runs, bats over .300 (.306 career), and averages over 20 steals per season. In 2001, the Texas Rangers offered him a record $25 million per season to leave the Mariners. In 2004, the Yankees bought out his contract, and Rodriguez began playing third base for them. Interestingly, New York fans seem to have a hard time embracing both Derek Jeter and Alex Rodriguez. But both contribute to the success of the Yankee franchise.

The Big Unit Is Scary!

In the 1993 all-star game, the Phillies' best hitter, left-hander John Kruk, stepped up against Randy Johnson for the first time. Kruk was completely intimidated. He ducked and backed away from three straight pitches—but all three were strikes.

Vladimir Gurrero

For eight years Gurrero played with the Montreal Expos, a team that languished at the bottom of the NL East, well away from the attention of the national media. In those years, though, Gurrero established himself as one of the best hitters of the era: he hit 30 to 40 home runs with a .300 plus batting average pretty much every year. In 2004 he signed with the Angels, where he earned the American League's MVP Award. His home country, the Dominican Republic, celebrated Gurrero's MVP award with a national holiday.

Other Great Hitters

There are many other great hitters in baseball today—too many to name them all. First baseman Derrek Lee had always been an excellent defender, but he blossomed as a hitter in 2005 with the Cubs. He came back in 2007 after an injury-plagued 2006. Joe Mauer of the Twins led his league in batting average—and he's a catcher! Red Sock Manny Ramirez may be a quirky guy, filling Boston newspapers with stories of "Manny being Manny," but he's one heck of a hitter, leading the AL in batting in 2002, and in homers in 2004. Designated hitters Travis Hafner of Cleveland and David Ortiz of Boston are the absolute best at their "position."

Of course, it's not just power that makes a hitter valuable to his team. Speedster Scott Podsednik of the White Sox causes trouble for pitchers every time he gets on base because he steals bases—he stole 70 in the 2004 season. (To be fair, he did hit a game-winning home run in the 2005 World Series, but who would've guessed?) The best defensive center fielder today is the Braves' Andruw Jones, who will chase down any ball hit his way, and can hit pretty well, too.

Keep watching. In another year or two, new superstar players are sure to emerge, and you will be able to say, "I saw him when he was a rookie!"

All-Time Greats Who Are Still Playing

A few players who are nearing the end of their careers belong in the list of the greatest players ever. Here they are, with stats as of the start of the 2007 season:

Randy Johnson, 1988–present Expos, Mariners, Astros, Diamondbacks, Yankees

W–L	ERA	K
280–147	3.22	4,544

The slender 6'10" Johnson has become known as "The Big Unit," as he fires the ball down at hitters who just try to see his fastball, much less hit it. Johnson came up to the big leagues with Montreal in 1988, but it was with the Seattle Mariners that he became the dominating pitcher that he is today. Between 1993 and 1997, Johnson posted a 75–20 win/loss record, had his first 300+ strikeout season, and picked up his first Cy Young Award. In 1998 he was traded to Houston and gave the National League a taste of what American League hitters had to deal with, a blazing fastball and tremendous control.

In 1999 he signed with the Arizona Diamondbacks. Over the next three seasons, through 2001, he posted 1,083 strikeouts (or an average of 361 per year) leading the league each time. With 372 strikeouts in 2001, he came just 11 short of the all-time record. He has led Arizona to the playoffs twice in their first four years as a team; he was joint MVP with Curt Schilling in the 2001 World Series. Johnson played with the Yankees for 2005 and 2006, but moved back to Arizona for the 2007 season.

Greg Maddux, 1986–present Cubs, Braves, Padres

W–L	ERA	K
333–203	3.07	3,169

He doesn't have the blazing fastball of Randy Johnson, and he doesn't put up amazing strikeout totals, but his secret to pitching is, as he puts it, "making your strikes look like balls and your balls look like strikes." Maddux is a very smart pitcher with tremendous control who knows how to get batters out. In 1997, for example, he walked only 14 batters in over 230 innings. He knows how to throw several pitches very well, mixes them up, and can hit the corners of the plate. In 1995 and '96, with the Braves, Greg went a combined 35–8 with a 1.60 ERA, capturing two of his four Cy Young Awards; in fact, some people in the late 1990s joked about renaming the award the "Greg Maddux Award." Maddux started his career with the Cubs, but they let him sign with the Braves after he won the Cy Young award in 1992. In 2004, after an amazing 11 years in Atlanta (including 10 division titles), he went back to the Cubs as a free agent; he signed with the Padres for the 2007 season.

Roger Clemens, 1984–present Red Sox, Blue Jays, Yankees, Astros

W–L	ERA	K
348–178	3.10	4,604

In 1986, a young Clemens led the Red Sox to the World Series, posting a 24–4 record while winning his first of a record seven Cy Young Awards. Clemens holds the record for most strikeouts in a game (20), which he accomplished twice.

"The Rocket," as he was nicknamed, was on his way to a tremendous career. Along with Greg Maddux, Clemens was

Seven MVPs!

In 2001, Barry Bonds became the first player to win four Most Valuable Player Awards. Then he won the award again in 2002, 2003, and 2004, giving him a record *seven* MVPs!

one of two active pitchers named to the All-Century Team of the 100 all-time greatest players of the 20th century. Clemens retired momentarily after pitching with the Yankees in the 2003 World Series. But his hometown Houston Astros made him an offer he couldn't refuse, so he came back in 2004 with them. Even though he was 42 years old, he still won his seventh Cy Young award, and helped the Astros come within a game of the World Series. In the last few seasons, Clemens has flirted with retirement, but he always seems to come back for one more season.

Barry Bonds, 1986–present Pirates, Giants

HR	RBI	AVG
734	1,930	.299

Barry's dad, Bobby, was a terrific player for the Giants and Yankees, but Barry has surpassed even dad's great ability. He hits for power, has a high average, stole bases in his younger days, and played great defense before his knees gave out. The young Bonds came up with the Pirates in 1986. By the 1990s he was a superstar. He was the most feared hitter in baseball in the early 1990s, winning the MVP in 1990, 1992, and 1993. In 2001, Bonds hit a single season record of 73 home runs. He led his San Francisco Giants to within one game of the World Series title in 2002. In 2005, Bonds, dogged with allegations of steroid use and having difficulty with his aging knees, sat out much of the season. He returned for both the 2006 and 2007 campaigns with the Giants. In 2007 he captured first place on the all-time home run list, surpassing Hank Aaron's record, but that achievement is unfortunately tainted by continued suspicions that Bonds used performance-enhancing drugs.

Ken Griffey Jr., 1989–present Mariners, Reds

HR	RBI	AVG
563	1,608	.291

Everyone calls him "Junior," and like Bonds, his dad was a major-league ballplayer. In fact, when he joined the majors in 1989 he played on the Seattle Mariners with his dad—the only time that's ever happened. Griffey, who genuinely loves to play the game, is one of the greatest center fielders ever, making many amazing catches and winning the Gold Glove for defense every year. He is a major home run threat as well and is often compared to the great Willie Mays. Griffey hit 56 home runs in 1997 and again in 1998 with over 140 RBIs each year. In 2000, he joined the Cincinnati Reds, the team on which his dad became famous. Unfortunately, injury after injury has slowed Junior down. He hit his 500th home run in 2004; Griffey was sixth on the all-time home run list at the beginning of the 2008 season, and he's still moving up fast.

Yogi Berra Quotes

Former Yankee Catcher Yogi Berra is known for his many unintentionally funny sayings. He said,

- "It ain't over 'til it's over."
- "Baseball is 90 percent mental; the other half is physical."
- "You can observe a lot just by watching."
- "Nobody goes to that restaurant anymore, it's too crowded."

Did Yogi really say all these things? Someone asked him, and he said: "I really didn't say everything I said."

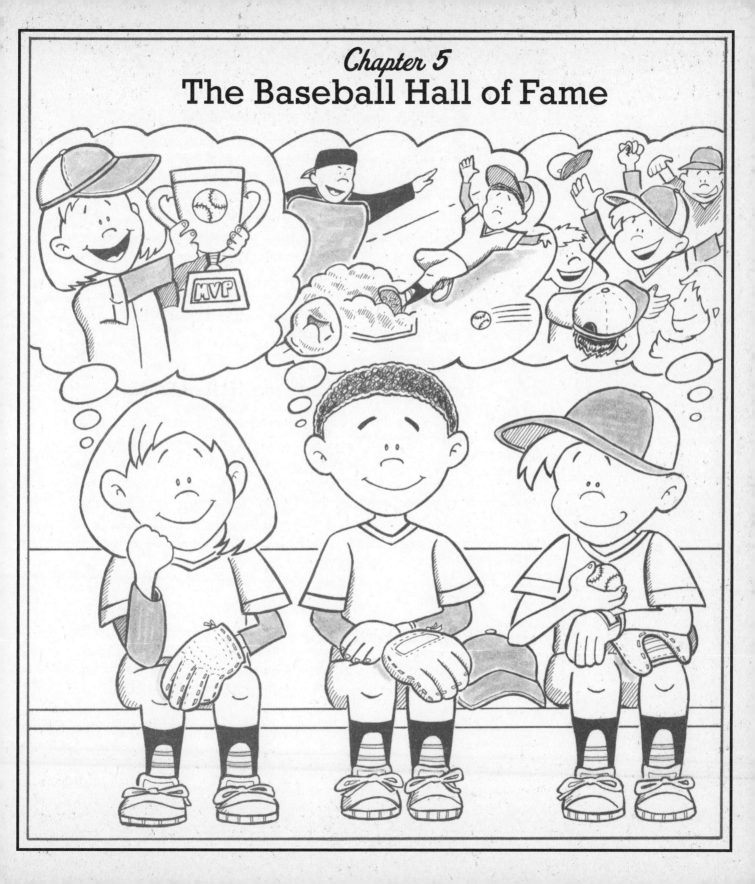

Chapter 5
The Baseball Hall of Fame

In 1936, the baseball community decided that they needed a place to honor the greatest players ever. Thus, the idea for the Hall of Fame was born. In June of 1939, the National Baseball Hall of Fame and Museum was opened in Cooperstown, New York. It's a place where you'll find bats and gloves used by the greatest players, balls that were hit for historic home runs, and plenty of other neat baseball stuff. The Hall includes plaques honoring the 260 members, which include 195 major-league players along with managers and other people closely associated with the game. There are even eight umpires included. Every fan should drop by for a visit!

How to Make It into the Hall of Fame

Making the Hall of Fame is a tremendous honor that only a small portion of baseball players ever receive. A player must be retired from baseball for five years before he is eligible to be elected to the Hall. Most players are voted in by baseball writers—writers can vote for up to 10 players on each year's ballot. A player who is voted for by three-fourths of the writers becomes a Hall-of-Famer. Generally only two or so players make the Hall of Fame each year.

Cooperstown

Popular Hall of Fame Exhibits

The three-floor Hall of Fame Museum has many exhibits in different rooms that honor different parts of the game.

- "The Great American Home Run Chase" pays tribute to the yearly chase to see if anyone can break the record for most home runs in a season. Featured are balls, bats, and other items from the only five players ever to hit more than 60 homers in one season: Babe Ruth, Roger Maris, Mark McGwire, Sammy Sosa, and Barry Bonds.

- The "Today's Stars" exhibit includes all sorts of information about the current stars of the game.
- "Baseball Around the World" gives fans a look at how baseball is played in other countries such as Japan and Cuba.
- A "No-Hitters" exhibit honors the pitchers who have pitched no-hit games throughout baseball history. Nolan Ryan, who pitched an incredible seven no-hitters, is prominently featured.
- "The World Series Room" has all sorts of displays and memorabilia from what is called "The Fall Classic," the World Series, where the best of the American League and the best of the National League meet every year to determine baseball's champion.
- "Hail to the Champs" honors the most recent World Series winners. This is a particularly fun place to visit if your favorite team won last year's championship.
- "The Evolution of Equipment" shows how bats, balls, gloves, catcher's masks, and uniforms have changed over the many years baseball has been played. You might be amazed at the huge difference in equipment a century ago.
- "Pride and Passion" is an exhibit honoring the African-American experience in baseball, including the Negro leagues and memorabilia from the great players, including Jackie Robinson.
- "Ballparks" has actual seats, dugout benches, and even turnstiles from many of the great ballparks that have been torn down and replaced by newer stadiums over the years.

Hall of Fame Quote

Pitcher Dizzy Dean once said something worthy of Yogi Berra: "The doctors X-rayed my head and found nothing."

There is much to see, including films and even an actual ball field where two major-league teams square off every summer in a special exhibition game. The Hall of Fame also has special programs that include "sandlot stories" about the game, movies, and book signings by some of the many authors who write about the game, which often include former players, managers, and popular broadcasters. There's even a daily scavenger hunt for kids to take part in during the summer months. You may have to move through the Hall of Fame slowly because (a) it's crowded, and (b) there's so much to check out!

A Little History of the Hall

The idea for the Hall of Fame began in Cooperstown in the 1930s. Cooperstown was where Abner Doubleday, who many credit with inventing the game, had lived, so it seemed to be the ideal place to build such a museum to honor the game. In 1936, as baseball approached its 100th anniversary, plans were made to honor the greatest players of the game. That year, the first five players, Ty Cobb, Babe Ruth, Honus Wagner, Christy Mathewson, and Walter Johnson, were voted in as the first players to make the Hall of Fame. By 1939, the actual building was completed. There was a big ceremony that summer, and the Hall of Fame was officially opened, displaying all sorts of stuff from the game to that point. It was a small museum at first, but thousands of people flocked to tiny Cooperstown to visit. Over the years the Hall has grown, with new wings added on to accommodate all of the new exhibits plus a gallery, a library, and more. Today, between 300,000 and 400,000 people visit the baseball shrine annually. That's quite a lot of visitors for a town whose year-long population is only 2,300 people.

Hall of Fame Quote

Ernie Banks, called "Mr. Cub," was the cheerful former shortstop and two-time MVP who loved to play so much that he became known for saying, "It's a great day for a ballgame. Let's play two."

Special Election

In 2006, a special one-time committee of baseball historians chose 17 players and executives from the Negro leagues to be inducted into the Hall of Fame.

The Baseball Hall of Fame

The Hall of Fame Players

Catchers

Johnny Bench	Carlton Fisk
Yogi Berra	Josh Gibson (Negro leagues)
Roger Bresnahan	
Roy Campanella	Gabby Hartnett
Gary Carter	Ernie Lombardi
Mickey Cochrane	Biz Mackey (Negro leagues)
Bill Dickey	Louis Santop (Negro leagues)
Buck Ewing	
Rick Ferrell	Ray Schalk

FUN FACT

Not the Yankees

Do you know which team has the most players in the Hall of Fame? It's not the Yankees; it's the Giants, with 24.

First Basemen

Cap Anson	Harmon Killebrew
Jake Beckley	Buck Leonard
Jim Bottomley	Willie McCovey
Dan Brouthers	Johnny Mize
Orlando Cepeda	Eddie Murray
Frank Chance	Tony Pérez
Roger Connor	George Sisler
Jimmie Foxx	Mule Suttles (Negro leagues)
Lou Gehrig	
Hank Greenberg	Ben Taylor (Negro leagues)
George Kelly	Bill Terry

Second Basemen

Rod Carew	Rogers Hornsby
Eddie Collins	Nap Lajoie
Bobby Doerr	Tony Lazzeri
Johnny Evers	Bill Mazeroski
Nellie Fox	Bid McPhee
Frankie Frisch	Joe Morgan
Charlie Gehringer	Jackie Robinson
Frank Grant (Negro leagues)	Ryne Sandberg
Billy Herman	Red Schoendienst

Shortstops

Luis Aparicio	Phil Rizzuto
Luke Appling	Joe Sewell
Dave Bancroft	Ozzie Smith
Ernie Banks	Joe Tinker
Lou Boudreau	Arky Vaughn
Joe Cronin	Honus Wagner
George Davis	Bobby Wallace
Travis Jackson	John Ward
Hugh Jennings	Willie Wells
Pop Lloyd	Robin Yount
Rabbit Maranville	
Pee Wee Reese	

Veteran's Committee: A special committee, separate from the baseball writers, votes in veterans of the game. After a player has been retired for 20 years, his name is removed from the writers' ballots, and he must be voted in by the Veteran's Committee. The Veteran's Committee can also vote in folks who didn't play in the majors, such as Negro leaguers, broadcasters, umpires, or executives.

What about Third Base?

There have been many great third baseman in baseball history, but only 13 have made the Hall of Fame, the fewest of any position.

Third Basemen

Frank "Home Run" Baker
Wade Boggs
George Brett
Jimmy Collins
Ray Dandridge
Judy Johnson (Negro leagues)
George Kell

Fred Lindstrom
Eddie Mathews
Brooks Robinson
Mike Schmidt
Pie Traynor
Jud Wilson (Negro leagues)

Outfielders

Hank Aaron
Richie Ashburn
Earl Averill
James "Cool Papa" Bell (Negro leagues)
Lou Brock
Willard Brown (Negro leagues)
Jesse Burkett
Max Carey
Oscar Charleston (Negro leagues)
Fred Clarke
Roberto Clemente
Ty Cobb
Earle Combs
Sam Crawford

Kiki Cuyler
Ed Delahanty
Joe DiMaggio
Larry Doby
Hugh Duffy
Elmer Flick
Goose Goslin
Chick Hafey
Billy Hamilton
Harry Heilmann
Harry Hooper
Pete Hill (Negro leagues)
Monte Irvin
Reggie Jackson
Al Kaline
Willie Keeler

Game Pieces

Baseball is such a familiar game that you might not even need words to describe it! Study the four picture puzzles below and see if you can figure out what baseball play, player, or place they each describe.

Joe Kelley
King Kelly
Ralph Kiner
Chuck Klein
Mickey Mantle
Heinie Manush
Willie Mays
Tommy McCarthy
Joe Medwick
Stan Musial
Jim O'Rourke
Mel Ott
Kirby Puckett
Sam Rice
Frank Robinson
Edd Roush
George Herman "Babe" Ruth
Al Simmons

Enos Slaughter
Duke Snider
Tris Speaker
Willie Stargell
Turkey Stearnes
Sam Thompson
Cristóbal Torriente (Negro leagues)
Lloyd Waner
Paul Waner
Zack Wheat
Billy Williams
Ted Williams
Hack Wilson
Dave Winfield
Carl Yastrzemski
Ross Youngs

Pitchers

Pete Alexander
Chief Bender
Mordecai Brown
Ray Brown (Negro leagues)
Jim Bunning
Steve Carlton
Jack Chesbro
John Clarkson
Andy Cooper (Negro leagues)
Stan Coveleski
Leon Day (Also 2B and OF)

Dizzy Dean
Martin Dihigo (Negro leagues)
Don Drysdale
Dennis Eckersley
Red Faber
Bob Feller
Rollie Fingers
Whitey Ford
Bill Foster
Pud Galvin
Bob Gibson

Lefty Gómez

Burleigh Grimes

Lefty Grove

Jesse Haines

Waite Hoyt

Carl Hubbell

Jim "Catfish" Hunter

Fergie Jenkins

Walter Johnson

Addie Joss

Tim Keefe

Sandy Koufax

Bob Lemon

Ted Lyons

Juan Marichal

Rube Marquard

Christy Mathewson

Joe McGinnity

José Méndez (Negro leagues)

Hal Newhouser

Kid Nichols

Phil Niekro

Satchel Paige (Negro leagues)

Jim Palmer

Herb Pennock

Gaylord Perry

Eddie Plank

Charley Radbourn

Eppa Rixey

Robin Roberts

Bullet Rogan

Red Ruffing

Amos Rusie

Nolan Ryan

Tom Seaver

Hilton Smith (Negro leagues)

Warren Spahn

Bruce Sutter

Don Sutton

Dazzy Vance

Rube Waddell

Ed Walsh

Mickey Welch

Hoyt Wilhelm

Joe Williams

Vic Willis

Early Wynn

Cy Young

Designated Hitters

Paul Molitor

How do you get to the Baseball Hall of Fame?

To find the answer, follow the correct path from PLAY BALL to GAME OVER. Collect the letters along the way, and write them in order on the lines below.

_ _ _ _ _ _ _ ' _ _ _ _ _ ' _ _ _ _ _ _ !

Chapter 6
Ballparks

WORDS to KNOW

Astroturf: In the 1970s, some fields were built with "Astroturf," which is a green plastic carpet that covers the field in place of grass. Astroturf was easier to take care of than grass, but it was ugly, and it caused strange bounces. Of course, permanently roofed stadiums (like the Metrodome or Tropicana Field, where the Devil Rays play) can't have natural grass; but virtually all other stadiums today now have natural grass rather than Astroturf.

foul pole: A ball that flies over the outfield fence is only a home run if it leaves the field in fair territory. The foul poles make it easy to tell whether a ball is a home run: One side of the pole is fair; the other is foul. But if the ball hits the foul pole, it's a home run.

I n baseball, like in most sports, some things need to be the same on every field. For example, the bases are always 90 feet apart, and the pitcher's mound is always 60 feet, 6 inches away from home plate. Unlike in other sports, though, some parts of baseball fields can be different. The distance from home plate to the outfield fences may be different from one park to another. The distance from the foul lines to the stands can vary. Some ballparks are indoors and others are outdoors. The home ballpark holds a special place in the heart of each team's fans. Fans who travel often like to attend games in as many parks as possible. This chapter offers descriptions of some of today's 30 major-league ballparks.

Classic Old Ballparks

Wrigley Field: *Chicago Cubs*

Opened: 1914
Capacity: 38,902
The Lowdown: Wrigley Field is more than a ballpark; it's a landmark in Chicago. The Cubs moved in back in 1926.
Features: Ivy-covered brick outfield walls, an old hand-operated scoreboard, and rooftop views from the surrounding apartment buildings.

Say What?

Yogi Berra was known as being quite a talker behind the plate. He hoped his chatter would distract the batter! The story goes that in the 1958 World Series, with the legendary Hank Aaron hitting, Yogi kept telling Aaron to "hit with the label up on the bat." Finally, Aaron couldn't stand it any more. He turned to Yogi and said "_____!"

To find out what Hank Aaron said to Yogi Berra, figure out where to put each of the cut apart pieces of the grid.

C'mon Hank, hit it with the label up. Up, up, up, with the label up. C'mon Hank, hit it with the label up...

Fenway Park: *Boston Red Sox*

Opened: 1912
Capacity: 34,218
The Lowdown: The oldest and smallest ballpark in the major leagues sits right in the heart of Boston.
Features: "The Green Monster" is the name given to the 37-foot-high green wall that is the left field fence. Inside the Monster is a hand-operated scoreboard, and high atop is a 23-foot netting that catches home runs before they fly onto the streets that surround the park. In 2003 seats were installed on top of the Green Monster.

Yankee Stadium: *New York Yankees*

Opened: 1923
Capacity: 67,000
Lowdown: They call it "The House That Ruth Built" in honor of the Babe. It's located in the Bronx, right off the #4 subway line.
Features: Monuments honoring Yankee greats sit in Monument Park, which is a mini Hall of Fame of sorts. There are even stadium tours of this classic ballpark, which is a must-see site for visitors to the city.

vendor: At most major-league stadiums, you can buy food or drinks without leaving your seat. Vendors walk through the aisles, shouting out what they have for sale: "Hot Dogs, get yer Hooooooooot Dogs Right HERE!" The call of the vendors is a memorable part of a major-league ballgame.

Dodger Stadium: *Los Angeles Dodgers*

Opened: 1962
Capacity: 56,000
The Lowdown: The park is located in Chavez Ravine, within sight of downtown Los Angeles and many freeways; however, the view past the outfield is of nothing but gorgeous palm trees on a mountain landscape.

Features: Right by the foul poles in left and right field, the outfield fence is only three feet high. During the game you can eat a world famous "Dodger Dog."

High in the Sky Ballpark

Coors Field: *Colorado Rockies*

Opened: 1995
Capacity: 50,381
The Lowdown: The ballpark sits over 5,000 feet above sea level where the air is thinner, which means that when the ball is hit it travels farther than at any other stadium. Hitters love Coors, while pitchers hate it.

Features: An old-fashioned clock tower greets fans at the entrance. A hand-operated scoreboard is inside the right field fence. A modern heating system under the field helps melt the snow—and Denver gets snow even during baseball season.

New Park, Old Look

Oriole Park at Camden Yards: *Baltimore Orioles*

Opened: 1992
Capacity: 48,262
The Lowdown: A new ballpark with an old-time flavor. People come from all over the east coast to check out the stadium and surrounding waterfront area. Camden Yards was the first of a long line of new ballparks built to mimic the charm of early 1900s baseball.

Features: An old-fashioned brick look on the outside and a giant building called the Warehouse overlooking the stadi-

Misplaced Foul Poles

When Dodger Stadium first opened in 1962, the foul poles didn't line up with the rest of the field. The team had to move home plate for the start of the next season for the field to be correctly aligned.

um give the park an old-time feeling. Inside the Warehouse is a gift shop and cafeteria.

Neat New Ballparks

PNC Park: *Pittsburgh Pirates*

Opened: 2001
Capacity: 38,496
The Lowdown: The view of the Roberto Clemente Bridge across the Allegheny River is breathtaking. This park was judged best in baseball by ESPN in 2005.
Features: The park only has two decks, so the highest seat is only 88 feet from the field.

Bank One Ballpark: *Arizona Diamondbacks*

Opened: 1998
Capacity: 48,569
The Lowdown: The stadium is right smack in the city of Phoenix.
Features: The field is natural grass, even though the stadium has a retractable roof. Fans can buy "seats" in the swimming pool behind the center field fence.

FUN FACT

Naming Rights

In many cities, companies have paid for the right to name the ballpark after their company. As a result, some parks have changed names. For instance, Houston's Enron Field became Minute Maid Park; Chicago's Comiskey Park became US Cellular Park; the Oakland Coliseum became McAfee Coliseum. Miami's Joe Robbie Stadium became Pro Player Stadium, but changed to Dolphins Stadium after the Pro Player company went out of business.

SBC Park: *San Francisco Giants*

Opened: 2000
Capacity 40,800
The Lowdown: The right field fence sits next to McCovey Cove on San Francisco Bay. Kayakers often paddle in the bay beyond the fence, hoping to catch a home run.

Features: Kids can play whiffle ball in a miniature version of the park behind the left field fence. There's a walkway along the waterfront where people can watch the game for free.

Hink Pinks

The answer to Hink Pinks are two rhyming words. Both words of the answer should have the same number of syllables. See if you can score four!

1. The heavier of two batters.

F _ _ _ _ _   B _ _ _ _ _

2. Where you throw a bad referee.

U _ _   D _ _ _

3. Nine baseball players shouting at once.

T _ _ _   S _ _ _ _ _ _

4. The last part of a baseball game when one team has more points.

W _ _ _ _ _ _   I _ _ _ _

97

Baseball Diamond

Can you find six common baseball terms hidden in the diamond grid? Start at a letter and move one space at a time in any direction to a touching letter. You may not use the same letter twice in a word, but you can cross over your own path.

HINT:
One of the terms is an abbreviation!

The Next Ballparks

It's fun to see games at the same ballpark where your parents orgrandparents used to root for the home team, but it's also exciting whenteams move to brand-new parks. A bunch of teams, including the MinnesotaTwins and the New York Yankees, have announced plans to build new parks. (The Twins will move out of the Metro-dome and into an open-air stadium inMinneapolis; the Yankees are building a new Yankee Stadium right next to thecurrent Yankee Stadium.) Make sure you keep current with ballpark news. Younever know where your favorite team might go next!

Chapter 7
The World Series

"T"he Fall Classic," as the World Series is often called, is the peak of the baseball season, when the best in the American League and the best in the National League square off for the championship of Major League Baseball. Many of baseball's greatest players have performed at their best in the Series; many of baseball's most memorable moments have occurred during the Series. But the World Series is more than a simple means of crowning a champion. It is a national event, a yearly cultural milepost that guides the memories of many Americans. This chapter gives an introduction to some of these memories.

Origins and History of the World Series

The World Series began in 1903, when the National League and the American League agreed to cooperate to crown an overall champion. Until 1969, the American and National League teams never met until the World Series. There were no playoffs, and just eight teams in each league. The team that won the most games in the season won their league's pennant; the two pennant winners would then play the World Series, starting right away after the end of the season. In 1969, when the leagues went to twelve teams each, they were divided into two divisions of six teams each, labeled East and West. The East and West champions played a playoff series to decide who would go to the World Series. Now there are thirty major-league teams and three divisions in each league (East, Central, and West), plus *two* rounds of playoffs. But no matter how they get there, the pennant-winning teams in each league meet in the World Series.

The Yankees, by far, have appeared in the most Fall Classics and won more than any other team. Between 1927 and 1964 the Yankees were almost always in the Series. As the 1900s came to an end, the Yankees put their stamp on the

World Series by winning titles in 1996, 1998, 1999, and 2000, giving them 26 titles overall.

Many of baseball's most memorable moments occurred in World Series games. Here are some highlights of notable World Series events.

1903: On September 16, the first World Series ever began between the Pittsburgh Pirates and the Boston Americans (who became the Boston Red Sox). The Americans won the Series 5 games to 3. Cy Young won two games.

1904: The World Series was not played, because the NL champion New York Giants refused to play the AL champion Boston Americans. The Giants said that the American League wasn't good enough to play with them. (That's funny, since Boston's American League team had beaten the NL's Pirates the previous year.)

1905: The New York Giants beat the Philadelphia A's 4 games to 1. All five games were shutouts. Christy Mathewson pitched an incredible three complete game shutouts and walked only one batter for the most amazing overall pitching performance in World Series history.

1908: The Chicago Cubs beat the Detroit Tigers 4 games to 1 to win their second title in a row. The Cubs have not won a World Series since.

1918: Babe Ruth won two games as a pitcher and the Red Sox won their third World Series in four years, beating the Cubs 4 games to 2. They didn't win another Series for 86 years.

1919: This year's White Sox team became known as the Black Sox after they lost the Series to the Reds, 5 games to 3, and were accused of losing the Series on purpose because they were paid money by gamblers. Eight White Sox players were banned from baseball for life.

1921: The Giants beat the Yankees 5 games to 3 in the first ever all–New York Series.

FUN FACT

Best of Seven

The World Series is played as a "best of seven" series: this means that the first team to win four games wins the Series, and there can't be more than seven games. In 1903, and again in 1918 through 1920, the Series was played as best of nine, but that was changed back to today's best-of-seven format.

The Babe Comes in Second

The Babe is not only second on the list of career home runs, but he has also hit the second-most World Series homers, 15. Mickey Mantle has hit the most Series homers, 18.

A Treasury of World Series Information

The Web site Baseball-almanac.com includes detailed summaries of every World Series, including box scores from each game.

Subway Series: In New York City, most people get from place to place via the subway. So, when two New York teams play each other in the Series, it's called a "Subway Series." The most recent Subway Series was in 2000, when the Yankees beat the Mets.

1936: The Yankees scored eighteen runs in Game 2 and thirteen runs in Game 6 en route to a 4–2 Series win over their across-the-river rivals, the Giants. It was the Yankees' first post-Ruth World Series and featured Lou Gehrig and Joe DiMaggio together for the first time in the post season.

1944: The first and only all–St. Louis World Series featured the Browns (who later became the Baltimore Orioles) against the Cardinals. A total of only 28 runs were scored by the two teams in a six-game Series won by the Cardinals 4–2.

1954: In a 2–2 opening game between the Giants and the Indians, Willie Mays made what may be baseball's most famous catch, running to the deepest part of center field and grabbing the ball with his back to home plate to keep the score tied. The Giants won the Series 4–0.

1955: After losing five times to the Yankees in the World Series, the Brooklyn Dodgers finally defeated the Yankees 4 games to 3 to win their only World Championship. Duke Snider hit four homers and Johnny Podres pitched two complete game victories, including a Game 7 shutout.

1956: In Game 5, Don Larsen of the Yankees pitched the only ever World Series perfect game. The Yankees won the Series over the Dodgers once again, this time in seven games, 4–3.

1960: Second baseman Bill Mazeroski hit a walk-off home run in the bottom of the ninth inning of the seventh game to give the underdog Pirates a win over the mighty Yankees.

1966: An amazing Orioles pitching staff shut the Dodgers out three consecutive times, including two 1–0 games, to complete a four-game sweep. The Dodgers had only two runs on seventeen hits.

The "Whole World" Series

While the World Series is played here in America, baseball is popular all over the world! See if you can match the country names with their location to fill in the grid. We left you the W-O-R-L-D S-E-R-I-E-S to help.

TOGO   MEXICO
PERU   ITALY
EGYPT   TAIWAN
IRAN   CANADA
COOK ISLANDS
PUERTO RICO
RUSSIA

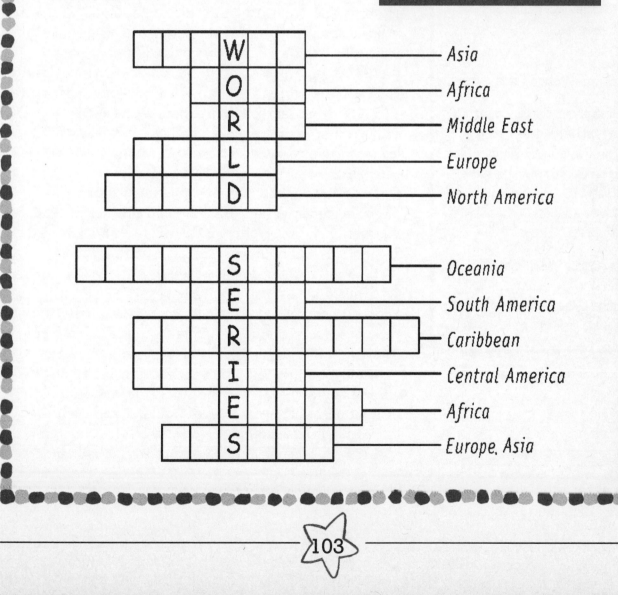

— Asia
— Africa
— Middle East
— Europe
— North America

— Oceania
— South America
— Caribbean
— Central America
— Africa
— Europe, Asia

1969: The team known as the worst in baseball for their first seven years, the Mets, came from nowhere to win 100 games in the regular season. Then they beat the favored Orioles 4–1 in the Series. Game 3 featured two amazing diving catches by Mets outfielder Tommie Agee.

1975: In the bottom of the 12th inning of Game 6, Red Sox Hall of Fame catcher Carleton Fisk hit a home run over Fenway Park's Green Monster to win the game, and to force a Game 7. The famous replay shows Fisk jogging down the first base line, trying to "push" his home run fair. The Reds won the seventh game and the Series, 4–3. Five games were decided by one run in this very close Series.

1977: Reggie Jackson hit three consecutive home runs in the sixth game to lead the Yankees to a 4–2 Series win over the LA Dodgers. Jackson hit five home runs and batted .450 in the Series. Based on this and other outstanding postseason performances, Reggie Jackson became known as "Mr. October."

1980: Tug McGraw struck out batters with the bases loaded in games 5 and 6 to secure two wins for the Phillies, who won their first World Series. Hall-of-Famers Steve Carlton and Mike Schmidt were Phillies heroes.

1986: After being down to their final out in Game 6, the Mets rallied in the tenth inning to beat the Red Sox when Mookie Wilson hit a ground ball through first baseman Bill Buckner's legs, scoring Ray Knight to force a seventh game. The Mets blew out the Sox in Game 7 to win the Series.

1988: An injured Kirk Gibson pinch hit a dramatic two-run walk-off homer to win the first game of the Series for the Dodgers over the favored Oakland A's. The homer started the Dodgers off on the way to a 4–1 Series win.

1989: This year's World Series pitted the Oakland A's against the San Francisco Giants. These cities are located across the San Francisco Bay from one another. Less than

Lots of Games

Catcher Yogi Berra of the Yankees played in the most World Series games ever, 75.

Seven Wins

Cardinals pitcher Bob Gibson won seven World Series games, even though his team made only three trips to the Series. In one game he struck out 17 batters.

Yikes

Pitcher George Frazier holds a dubious Yankee World Series record. In 1981 he lost three of the four games the Yankees lost to the Dodgers.

an hour before Game 2 was to begin, a terrible earthquake hit the area, causing all kinds of damage. Game 2 was postponed, but a week later, the cities and baseball decided to continue with the Series. The A's beat the Giants 4–0 in the Earthquake Series.

1993: For only the second time in World Series history, the Series ended on a game-winning home run. This homer came off the bat of Toronto Blue Jay's slugger Joe Carter, who gave the Jays an 8–6 win in the sixth and final game.

1995: The Atlanta Braves won 13 straight division titles between 1991 and 2004, making it to the World Series five times. But the Braves only won one of those, in 1995, when they beat the Indians in six games.

1999: The Yankees won their third title in four years and secured their place as team of the decade, beating the Braves 4–0. It was the fourth time in seven years the Braves lost the World Series.

2001: The World Series between the Arizona Diamond-backs and the New York Yankees started a week later than planned because baseball took a week off after the attacks on the World Trade Center and the Pentagon in September. The country suddenly was at war, yet baseball continued.

Games 3, 4, and 5 were played at Yankee Stadium below a torn flag pulled from the wreckage of the World Trade Center, and with President George W. Bush on hand. The Yankees twice pulled off improbable comeback victories: In game four, first baseman Tino Martinez hit a homer in the bottom of the ninth to tie the game, and then shortstop Derek Jeter hit the game-winning homer in the bottom of the tenth. In Game 5, third baseman Scott Brosius hit a walk-off home run in the bottom of the ninth to send the series back to Arizona. The Diamondbacks won Game 6 in a blowout; then they rallied in the bottom of the ninth in Game 7 to win on a bloop RBI single by Luis Gonzalez.

WORDS to KNOW

walk-off home run: When a player on the home team hits a home run in the bottom of the last inning that wins the game, that player's team can walk off the field after the runs score—the game is over. So, this kind of home run is called a "walk-off" home run.

FUN FACT

Bucky Dent

At the end of the 1978 season the Yankees and the Red Sox were tied for first place in the American League East. They played one game to decide which team went to the playoffs. The Yankees shortstop, Bucky Dent, hit only five home runs all season. But he hit the biggest homer of his career to win the game for the Yankees and to extend the Curse of the Bambino.

FUN FACT

Hard Luck Teams

Through most of your lifetime, even through your parents and grandparents' lifetimes, major-league baseball has told the story of three hard-luck teams: the Red Sox, the White Sox, and the Cubs. These teams had been good back in the 1900s and 1910s, but hadn't won a championship since then. All of a sudden, though, luck seems to have changed: the Red Sox won in 2004; the White Sox won in 2005. Could the Cubs be next?

2002: The San Francisco Giants led the Anaheim Angels 3 games to 2. In Game 6 the Giants were ahead 5–0 in the seventh inning, but the Angels came back to win, 6–5. In Game 7, the Angels took an early 4–1 lead and coasted from there to the championship.

2003: The Yankees once again represented the American League in the Series, but this time their veteran pitching couldn't top the Florida Marlins' young starters. The Yankees' four starters—David Wells, Andy Pettitte, Mike Mussina, and Roger Clemens—had started 15 World Series games. The Marlins' four starters—Mark Redman, Brad Penny, Carl Pavano, and Josh Beckett—had never been to the World Series. The Marlins triumphed in six games, the last a complete game shutout by Beckett.

2004: The Boston Red Sox broke the Curse of the Bambino by winning their first World Series since 1918. The World Series itself, in which Boston swept the St. Louis Cardinals 4–0, was almost anticlimactic after both League Championship Series. In the National League, the Cardinals, led by superstar Albert Pujols, beat the Houston Astros and 40-year-old Roger Clemens in an intense, exciting seven-game series. But the American League Championship Series, a reprise of the 2003 Yankees vs. Red Sox battle, captured most of the country's attention. The Yankees took a 3–0 lead in the series; no team in baseball history had ever come back to win a best-of-seven series after being down 3–0. But the Red Sox did it. They won two games in extra innings, each ending well after midnight. Curt Schilling pitched two games, even though one of his ankles was so injured that it bled visibly during the game. The Sox put away Game 7 early, taking an insurmountable lead on Johnny Damon's grand slam home run. All Boston fans know that crushing the hated Yankees in this manner would have been enough. But the Sox kept their momentum and steamrolled the power-hitting Cardinals in four games,

Name Change

In 1919, the Chicago White Sox were accused of being paid to lose the World Series! After that, the team became known by another name. Fill in all the letters that are not W-H-I-T-E to find out what it was.

BWLHAICTKESOX

capping the most exciting (if the most drawn-out) postseason in recent history.

2005: The Houston Astros made their first World Series appearance since they were founded in 1962. Their opponent was the Chicago White Sox, who had been around a lot longer, but had not won the Series since 1917. Both teams could attribute their success to their pitching staffs, especially their starting pitchers. In fact, in the American League Championship series, the White Sox only used one relief pitcher in the entire five-game series.

Game 3 in Houston turned into a marathon. In the middle of the night, way past even your parents' bedtime, Geoff Blum of the White Sox hit a fourteenth-inning home run that stood up for the win. The White Sox finished their

The Closer

Yankee relief pitcher John Wetteland became the first pitcher ever to save all four wins for his team in the 1996 World Series against Atlanta.

sweep of the Astros the next night, when series MVP Jermaine Dye drove in the only run of the game with an eighth-inning single.

2006: Just three years ago, the Detroit Tigers were the laughing stock of baseball, finishing with the second-worst season record ever. But in 2006, their talented young pitching staff dominated American League opposition. It seemed like the Tigers were on a roll to the championship. Their NL opponent was the St. Louis Cardinals, who squeaked into the postseason with a weak record in a weak division. Aside from superstar Albert Pujols, and former Cy Young winner Chris Carpenter, the Cardinals seemed more gritty than good.

In the World Series, though, it was the Cardinals who dominated. MVP shortstop David Eckstein, whom many thought was too small and too weak-armed to play in the majors, not only hit .364, but also anchored a solid defense that led the team to victory. Pitcher Jeff Weaver, who had been released earlier in the year for poor performance, made two solid starts and was the winning pitcher in the decisive Game 5. It helped the Cardinals that the Tigers defense made eight errors in five games.

2007: A stacked Red Sox team dominated the Colorado Rockies to sweep their way to the Sox' second title of the century. The Red Sox led the AL east for virtually the entire year. They were challenged in the ALCS by the Indians, who took a 3–1 lead, but behind the pitching of Josh Beckett, and the suddenly amazing bat of J.D. Drew, the Sox won their last seven postseason games. The Rockies were not an unworthy opponent. In perhaps the most incredible regular season finish ever, they went 14–1 over the season's last few weeks just to make the playoffs. Then, the Rockies swept the division series and the NLCS. Their luck ran out, though, when they went up against the Red Sox, who proved themselves to be one of the best baseball teams in existence.

Chapter 8
Statistics and Records

STATS, LLC.

STATS, LLC. is a company that maintains baseball statistics. They have reporters at every game who record the result of every pitch. Each year they publish several books filled with stats and scouting reports of current players.

Statistics are very much a part of baseball—more than in any other sport. Since the beginning of the sport, fans have wanted to know who had the most hits, who made the error, who got the win, and so on. Home run totals, batting averages, wins, strikeouts—they are all a central part of baseball's popularity. Sometimes when a player was on the verge of breaking a record, like when Cal Ripken Jr. played in his 2,131st game, or when Hank Aaron hit home run number 715, the individual achievements of the players got more attention than the ballgame. That's part of what makes baseball so interesting. Your team may not be doing well, like the Giants in 2006, but you might want to watch them to see a slugger like Barry Bonds pile up home runs on his way to a record.

Individual Stats

Players' individual statistics, or "stats," are followed closely, not only by fans but also by sportswriters, team management, and everyone associated with baseball. There are actually thousands of statistics that are recorded, from how long it took to play a game to how many times a hitter grounded out to the shortstop. Many baseball stats, such as batting average or runs batted in, have been kept and published since the late 19th and early 20th century. Others, like saves and holds, have been devised in more recent years. Computers now allow quick calculation of somewhat more obscure statistics, such as slugging percentage, or batting average with runners in scoring position. Below are the most common player statistics that you will see in the sports pages. They are usually found for each game in what was termed back in the 1800s as a "box score," or a summary of the game in a box. Over 100 years later, whether you find box scores in the newspaper or online, they are still the most popular way to see what happened in a ballgame.

Box Score

On Saturday, October 2, 2004, the Dodgers and the Giants were fighting for first place in the NL East and a playoff spot. The Dodgers trailed 3–0 entering the ninth inning; but they came back to win, the decisive runs coming on Steve Finley's walk-off grand slam home run. This victory clinched the division title for the Dodgers.

Box Scores				
Team	1 2 3	4 5 6	7 8 9	R H E
San Francisco Giants	0 0 0	2 0 0	1 0 0	3 6 2
Los Angeles Dodgers	0 0 0	0 0 0	0 0 7	7 7 0

San Francisco Giants 7, Los Angeles Dodgers 3

	123	456	789	RHE
Giants	000	200	100	362
Dodgers	000	000	007	770

Giants

NAME, Pos	ab	r	h	rbi	bb	avg
Durham, 2b	5	0	1	0	0	.280
Tucker, rf	4	0	0	0	1	.256
Alfonzo, 3b	4	0	1	0	0	.289
Snow, 1b	4	1	2	0	0	.327
Cruz, ss	4	0	0	0	0	.293
Ransom, ss	0	0	0	0	0	.258
Pierzynski, c	3	0	0	0	1	.270
Hermanson, p	0	0	0	0	0	.100
Christiansen, p	0	0	0	0	0	.000
Herges, p	0	0	0	0	0	.000
Franklin, p	0	0	0	0	0	.333
Grissom, cf	3	1	2	3	1	.277
Tomko, p	3	0	0	0	1	.113
Eyre, p	0	0	0	0	0	.000
Torrealba, c	0	0	0	0	0	.228
Totals	31	3	6	3	6	

Dodgers

NAME, Pos	ab	r	h	rbi	bb	avg
Izturis, ss	5	1	0	1	0	.288
Werth, lf	5	1	2	1	0	.266
Finley, cf	5	1	2	4	0	.271
Beltre, 3b	4	0	0	0	0	.335
Green, rf	4	1	2	0	0	.266
Ventura, 1b	3	1	0	0	1	.243
Cora, 2b	2	0	0	0	2	.264
Mayne, c	2	0	0	0	0	.221
Grabowski, ph	1	0	0	0	0	.219
Ross, c	0	0	0	0	0	.172
Hernandez, ph	0	1	0	0	1	.287
Dessens, p	1	0	0	0	0	.182
Alvarez, p	1	0	0	0	0	.161
Sanchez, p	0	0	0	0	0	.250
Venafro, p	0	0	0	0	0	.000
Carrara, p	0	0	0	0	0	.000
Saenz, ph	1	0	1	0	0	.282
Flores, pr	0	0	0	0	0	.000
Brazoban, p	0	0	0	0	0	.000
Choi, ph	0	0	0	1	1	.253
Perez, pr	0	1	0	0	0	.300
Totals	34	7	7	7	5	

E—Grissom, Ransom. LOB—San Francisco 8, Los Angeles 7. GIDP—Pierzynski. HR—Grissom (21), Finley (36). S—Torrealba.

Pitchers

San Francisco

NAME	ip	h	r	er	bb	so	era
Tomko	7.1	4	0	0	2	4	4.04
Eyre	0.1	0	0	0	0	0	4.10
Hermanson (L, 6–9)	0.2	1	4	4	3	1	4.53
Christiansen	0	0	1	0	0	0	4.50
Herges	0	1	1	1	0	0	5.23
Franklin	0	1	1	1	0	0	6.39

Los Angeles

NAME	ip	h	r	er	bb	so	era
Dessens	4	3	2	2	3	3	4.46
Alvarez	2	0	0	0	1	0	4.03
Sanchez	0.1	2	1	1	0	1	3.38
Venafro	.01	0	0	0	0	0	4.00
Carrara	1.1	1	0	0	1	1	2.18
Brazoban (W, 6–2)	1	0	0	0	1	0	2.48

Umpires: HP—McClelland, 1b—Randazzo, 2b—Culbreth, 3b—Wolf. Time of game: 3:40. Attendance: 46,005

The Ultimate Inning

In 1999, Fernando Tatis of the St. Louis Cardinals hit a grand slam home run. His team kept on hitting and scoring runs in the inning so that he got to bat again in the same inning with the bases loaded. Believe it or not, he hit another grand slam, becoming the first player ever to hit two grand slam home runs and drive in eight runs in one inning. Wow!

R, H, and E are runs, hits, and errors for each team for the game.

The rest of the abbreviations are as follows:

Pos is the position that player played. Sometimes a backup will take over at that position, like on the Giants' side where you see Cruz at shortstop (ss) replaced by Ransom.

The positions are:

1b	First base
2b	Second base
3b	Third base
ss	Shortstop
lf	Left fielder
cf	Center fielder
rf	Right fielder
c	Catcher
p	Pitcher
ph	Pinch hitter (someone who bats for another player, such as Saenz or Choi in the game above)
pr	Pinch runner (someone who runs for someone else, such as Flores in the game above)
dh	In the American League and in some minor leagues there are designated hitters, who bat for the pitchers.

The rest of the stats tell you what each player did in the game.

ab	At bats, or how many times the batter officially had a turn at bat (walks, sacrifices, and being hit by a pitch don't count as official at bats)
r	Runs scored
h	Hits

rbi	Runs batted in (a hit or another play that brings in a run or more)
bb	Base on balls (or walks)
so	Strikeouts, also sometimes listed as "k"
avg	Batting average

BUT what does it all mean, you may wonder. Well, it's very simple once you learn about the format.

Across the top is the inning-by-inning account of runs scored. You'll see that the Giants got 2 in the top of the fourth and another in the top of the seventh inning, but the Dodgers got 7 in the bottom of the ninth.

There will also be some information listed underneath the line that says "totals," telling you who hit doubles (2B), triples (3B), and home runs (HR) and how many the player has for the season in each category. You'll also see if a player had a sacrifice (S) or a sacrifice fly (SF), or if he grounded into a double play (GIDP). Players don't like to see it, but there is also a listing of errors (E) as well. Stolen bases (SB) and caught stealing (CS) are listed next. Some box scores may give you more detailed information, but these are the basics.

Pitching statistics are also included. Commonly you'll find next to pitchers' names first the "decision," meaning the win (W) or loss (L), or the save (S) for a reliever. In the game above, Brazoban was the winning pitcher in relief of Dessens, and no save was credited. Hermanson was the losing pitcher, also in relief. His win-loss record is listed as 6–9, or six wins and nine losses for the season.

batting average: A player's batting average is a good measure of his ability to hit. The best hitters have a .300 average or better. A player hitting .200 might be sent back to the minor leagues; no one has hit .400 for an entire season since Ted Williams hit .406 in 1941. To calculate a batting average, divide a player's hits by his at-bats.

I'll Play Anywhere

Only two players in baseball history have played all 10 positions. That's right, 10 ... Bert Campaneris of the A's and Cesar Tovar of the Twins not only played all nine defensive positions, including one pitching appearance each, but they were also designated hitters.

Other numbers you may see next to the name are:

bs   Blown saves, and a number of how many the pitcher has blown.

h   Hold, a new statistic, will show up for relief pitchers that says they held the lead until the closer came in and finished the game.

Then you'll see what is called the "pitcher's line," which includes:

ip   Innings pitched. Sometimes you'll see or 7.1, meaning the pitcher lasted seven innings and got one out in the eighth. 7.2 would mean he got two outs in the eighth.

h   Hits allowed

r   Runs allowed

er   Earned runs allowed. A run can be scored that doesn't count as an "earned run" because there was an error on the play that put the runner on base who later scored or helped the runner to score. In the game above the errors didn't allow any runs to score, so all runs were earned.

bb   Base on balls, or walks allowed

so   Strikeouts (sometimes listed as "k")

era   The up-to-date earned run average of the pitcher, or how many earned runs he allows per nine innings. Pitchers try to keep their earned run averages under 4.00, which is getting harder to do in recent years. Under 3.50 is quite good and under 3.00 is excellent. Starting pitchers pitch more innings, so it's harder for them to keep those ERAs down.

Now check out the newspaper, or your favorite online sports site, to find more box scores. Even if you didn't watch or listen to the game, you can figure out what happened, or what your favorite player did. Reading box scores is the best way to stay up-to-date with what's happening in major-league baseball.

Player Statistics

If you turn over baseball cards or look at numerous baseball books, including this one, you'll find ballplayers' statistics for each season and for their careers.

The most commonly found stats for hitters include:

G	Games played
AB	At-bats
R	Runs
H	Hits
2B	Doubles
3B	Triples
HR	Home runs
RBI	Runs batted in
BB	Base on balls (also known as walks)
K or SO	Strikeouts
AVG	Batting average
SB	Stolen bases
CS	Caught stealing

You might also see SLG, or slugging percentage, which takes one point for each single, two for each double, three for each triple, and four for each home run, adds them up and divides by the number of at bats. Unlike batting averages, which rarely top .350, slugging percentages for the best power hitters can reach .600 or higher.

Common pitching stats include:

W	Wins
L	Losses
PCT	This is winning percentage, or how often the pitcher gets a

FuN FACT

Shutouts

A pitcher earns a shutout by holding the opposing team without a run for the whole game. The pitcher who threw the most shutouts in baseball history was Walter Johnson, "The Big Train," who blanked the other team 110 times in his career.

WORDS to KNOW

assist: When a player makes a throw of any kind to get an out, whether it's an infielder throwing a batter out at first base or an outfielder throwing out a runner at home plate, the fielder gets credit for an assist.

putout: The fielder who steps on the base or applies a tag to actually put the runner out gets credit for a putout.

fielding percentage: One measure of a fielder's strength is the fielding percentage. To calculate this stat, add the player's putouts and assists. Then, divide by the total of the player's putouts, assists, and errors. A good fielder will have a fielding percentage of .980 or .990. Outfielders are expected to have higher fielding percentages than infielders.

win versus a loss. Add together wins and losses, then take the number of wins and divide it by the number you get. For example, if a pitcher has a win-loss record of 10 wins and 2 losses, you would add 10 + 2 = 12. Then divide the 10 wins by 12 and you'll get .833, or a great winning percentage of .833!

G	Games pitched in
GS	Games started
CG	Complete games
Sho	Shutouts (held the opposing team to no runs)
IP	Innings pitched
Hits	Hits allowed
BB	Base on balls allowed
K or SO	Strikeouts
ERA	Earned run average

And for relief pitchers the most common two stats are:

S	Saves
BS	Blown saves

Beyond those found that we have listed, there are statistics kept for nearly everything, and you can find books that get more detailed depending on how much you love baseball statistics.

The same statistics listed for a player can also be found for a team.

Lucky Numbers

Baseball is a game full of numbers. There's the RBI and ERA numbers, the numbers on the scoreboard, and of course the lucky number on the shirt of your favorite player!

In this tricky little puzzle, you must figure out what lucky combination of numbers to use so that each column (up and down) or row (across) adds up to the right totals shown in the white numbers. The white arrows show you in which direction you will be adding. Lucky you—four numbers are in place to get you started!

Here are the rules:

- You are only adding the numbers in any set of white boxes that are touching each other.
- Use only the numbers 1 through 9. Each number can only be used *once* in each set.
- Remember that each answer has to be correct both across *and* down!

The Standings

To follow your favorite team, you can look in the newspaper at the sports pages or on a Web site like *www.mlb.com* and you can get plenty of information including the standings, the listings of who's in first place, second place, and so on.

The major leagues today are each broken into three divisions:

American League

East	Central	West
Baltimore Orioles	Chicago White Sox	Anaheim Angels
Boston Red Sox	Cleveland Indians	Oakland Athletics
New York Yankees	Detroit Tigers	Seattle Mariners
Tampa Bay Devil Rays	Kansas City Royals	Texas Rangers
Toronto Blue Jays	Minnesota Twins	

National League

East	Central	West
Atlanta Braves	Chicago Cubs	Arizona Diamondbacks
Florida Marlins	Cincinnati Reds	Colorado Rockies
Montreal Expos	Houston Astros	Los Angeles Dodgers
New York Mets	Milwaukee Brewers	San Diego Padres
Philadelphia Phillies	Pittsburgh Pirates	San Francisco Giants
	St. Louis Cardinals	

Other Columns You May See in the Standings Chart

- **Division:** the team's record against teams in their own division
- **Home/Road:** the team's record when playing at their home park, and the team's record when playing away from home
- **Interleague:** the team's record in games against the other league
- **Streak:** how many games the team has won or lost in a row
- **Last 10:** the team's record in their last 10 games

When you look at the standings in the papers, you'll see how many wins and losses the team has and their winning percentage, meaning what percentage of all the games they've played they've won.

Record Holders and Top Ten Lists

As mentioned earlier, there are statistics kept for everything in baseball. You could probably find the answer to "What pitcher threw the most wild pitches in night games at Wrigley Field in the 1940s?" Okay, so that's a trick question—there were no night games at Wrigley in the 1940s because they had no lights. The point is, however, that if you love statistics you could probably spend a year looking at baseball statistics and never see the same one twice.

Following are some favorites.

Secret Signals

Use the decoder to figure out what message the catcher signaled to the pitcher when the crab came up to bat.

A   G   N   S

C   H   O   T

E   I   P   U

F   L   R   Y

—

!

All-Time Record Holders as of the End of 2007

Back-to-Back No-Hitters!

The only pitcher ever to throw no-hitters in two starts in a row was Johnny Vander Meer of the Cincinnati Reds in 1938.

Hitting

Top 10 All-Time Home Run Leaders
1. Barry Bonds 762*
2. Hank Aaron 755
3. Babe Ruth 714
4. Willie Mays 660
5. Sammy Sosa 609*
6. Ken Griffey 593*
7. Frank Robinson 586
8. Mark McGwire 583
9. Harmon Killebrew 573
10. Rafael Palmeiro 569

*active player total at the start of the 2008 season
There are 20 players who have topped 500 home runs in their careers.

Top 10 All-Time RBI Leaders
1. Hank Aaron 2,297
2. Babe Ruth 2,213
3. Cap Anson 2,076
4. Lou Gehrig 1,995
5. Stan Musial 1,951
6. Ty Cobb 1,938
7. Jimmie Foxx 1,922
8. Eddie Murray 1,917
9. Willy Mays 1,903
10. Mel Ott 1,860

FUN FACT

Consecutive Scoreless Innings

Dodgers pitcher Orel Hershiser threw 59 straight innings without giving up a run in September of 1988, breaking Dodger Don Drysdale's previous record.

Manager Wins

The manager with the most all-time wins is Connie Mack, who won 3,731 games over 53 years between 1894 and 1950. His record has a lot to do with the many years he was a manager—he actually lost more games than he won!

Top Ten Batting Average Leaders (a player must have more than 5,000 at-bats to qualify for this list)

1. Ty Cobb .366
2. Rogers Hornsby .358
3. Ed Delahanty .346
4. Tris Speaker .345
5. Billy Hamilton .344
   Ted Williams .344
6. Dan Brouthers .342
7. Harry Heilmann .342
8. Babe Ruth .342
9. Willie Keeler .341
10. Bill Terry .345

Most Hits: Pete Rose at 4,256, followed by Ty Cobb at 4,191. They are the only two players with over 4,000 hits!

Most Grand Slam Home Runs: Lou Gehrig 23
Most Stolen Bases: Rickey Henderson 1,395
Most At-Bats: Pete Rose 14,053
Most Seasons Played: Nolan Ryan 27

Pitching

Top 10 All-Time Wins Leaders

1. Cy Young 511
2. Walter Johnson 417
3. Grover Alexander 373
4. Christy Mathewson 373
5. Pud Gavin 365
6. Warren Spahn 363
7. Kid Nichols 361
8. Tim Keefe 342
9. Steve Carlton 329
10. John Clarkson 328

Top 10 All-Time Strikeout Leaders

1. Nolan Ryan 5,174
2. Roger Clemens 4,672*
3. Randy Johnson 4,616*
4. Steve Carlton 4,136
5. Bert Blyleven 3,701
6. Tom Seaver 3,640
7. Don Sutton 3,574
8. Gaylord Perry 3,534
9. Walter Johnson 3,509
10. Phil Neikro 3,342

***Active player total at the start of the 2008 season.**

Lowest All-Time ERA (2,000 or more innings):
Ed Walsh 1.82
Most All-Time Saves: Lee Smith 478 (since 1969 when saves became an official statistic)
Most No-Hitters: Nolan Ryan 7

One-Season Records

Hitting

Most Doubles: Earl Webb 67, Boston Red Sox 1931
Most Triples: Chief Wilson 36, Pittsburgh Pirates 1912
Most Home Runs:

1. Barry Bonds 73, San Francisco Giants 2001
2. Mark McGwire 70, St. Louis Cardinals 1998
3. Sammy Sosa 66, Chicago Cubs 1998
4. Mark McGwire 65, St. Louis Cardinals 1999
5. Sammy Sosa 64, Chicago Cubs 2001
6. Sammy Sosa 63, Chicago Cubs 1999

How come Drew never finishes a baseball game?

To find out, cross out all the words that have three letters or the letter U!

AND	EVERY	CAT
TIME	GOT	HE
BAT	GETS	FAR
TO	FUR	THIRD
BUT	BASE	HIT
HE	HAT	GOES
HUT	HOME	BAG

7. Roger Maris 61, New York Yankees 1961
8. Babe Ruth 60, New York Yankees 1927
9. Babe Ruth 59, New York Yankees 1921
10. Jimmie Foxx 58, Philadelphia Athletics 1932
    Hank Greenberg 58, Detroit Tigers 1938
    Ryan Howard 58, Philadelphia Phillies 2006
    Mark McGwire 58, St. Louis Cardinals 1997

Most Runs Batted In: Hack Wilson 191, Chicago Cubs 1930
Most Hits: Ichiro Suzuki 262, Seattle Mariners 2004
Highest Batting Average (500+ Plate Appearances): Hugh Duffy .438, Boston Beaneaters 1894
Highest Average (500+ Plate Appearances) since 1900: Rogers Hornsby .424, St. Louis Cardinals 1924
Most Stolen Bases: Rickey Henderson 130, Oakland Athletics 1982

Pitching

Most Wins: Jack Chesbro 41, New York Highlanders 1904
Most Strikeouts: Nolan Ryan 383, California Angels 1973; Sandy Koufax 382, Los Angeles Dodgers, 1965
Lowest Earned Run Average: Dutch Leonard 1.01, Boston Red Sox 1914
Most Shutouts: Grover Alexander 16, Philadelphia Phillies 1916
Most Saves: Bobby Thigpen 57, Chicago White Sox 1990

Keeping score is a fun way to keep track of what's happening on the field, as well as to have a lasting record of the game you watched. Scorecards are sold at the ballpark, or you can make your own on a sheet of paper. The most important thing is that you have a place to write the name of each player and boxes for all nine innings (or more) so that you can put down what they do with each at-bat. Names run down the left side of the page and innings run across the top. Why not try scoring the next game you go to?

Scoring Symbols

Scoring is pretty easy once you know the symbols to put in the boxes. You are writing down what the batter does each time he bats. Most of the time you will be listing hits or outs. When the batter makes an out, he either hit the ball to a fielder, or he struck out. For scoring purposes, the fielders are numbered—this number has nothing to do with the numbers the players are wearing on their uniforms, but rather describes the position played by each player:

Numbers for fielding:
1. **Pitcher**
2. **Catcher**
3. **First baseman**
4. **Second baseman**
5. **Third baseman**
6. **Shortstop**
7. **Left fielder**
8. **Center fielder**
9. **Right fielder**

You write the number of the player or players who caught the ball to get the batter out. For example, if the ball

HOME OF THE DIGITS!

is hit in the air to the center fielder and he makes the catch for an out, you put "8" in the box. If the ball went to right field, you'd put "9," or to left field, "7." If the player pops it up and it's caught by the first baseman, you'd put "3," or for the second baseman you'd put "4," and so on. A line drive to the first baseman could be scored "3L."

If the ball is hit on the ground to the shortstop and he throws to first, you put down both numbers since they were both part of the play. Therefore a groundout to shortstop would be 6-3. A groundout to second base would be 4-3, a groundout to third base 5-3. If the first baseman picked up a groundball and the pitcher came over to cover first base, caught the throw, and stepped on the base for the out, it would be scored 3-1, because the first baseman is "3" and the pitcher is "1." A double play that goes from the shortstop to the second baseman to the first baseman would be scored DP 6-4-3.

Whatever fielders are involved in making the out are included in your scoring. Once you memorize the fielders' numbers it becomes very easy.

Hits can be scored in a few ways. A single is either "1B" or a single line (–), a double is "2B" or a double line (=), a triple is 3B or a triple line (≡), and a home run is "HR" or four lines (≡).

When runners get on base you keep track of them using the diamond in the box on the scorecard.

Just draw on the line for each base they get to. For example, if a player reaches first base you would draw the line going from home to first base. If the next player gets a single and that player moves to second base you would darken the line going from first base to second base.

As the players move around the bases you draw the lines of the diamond to follow them. Therefore, for every run scored you make a complete diamond.

WORDS to KNOW

pickoff: If the pitcher throws to a base and gets the runner out before he can get back to the base, it's called a pickoff. To score a pickoff at first base, write PO 1-3, meaning pickoff, pitcher to first baseman.

intentional walk: Sometimes the pitcher walks a batter on purpose; this is called an intentional walk. Sometimes an intentional walk makes it easier to get a double play; other times, the pitcher walks a good hitter so as to pitch to a weaker hitter later in the line-up. Score an intentional walk as "IW" or "IBB."

How to Score Hits

On the sample scorecard on page 137, how a batter reached base is written outside the diamond. However, some people prefer to write how the batter reached in the *middle* of the diamond. Either way works—do whatever makes sense to you.

commentators: The commentators are the people who describe the game for the radio or television audience. They must keep detailed scorecards so they can tell the audience what has happened in the game.

There are many, many variations on scoring. Sportswriters, broadcasters, fans, and people who are keeping the statistics for the team are all keeping score, and they're all doing it in a slightly different manner from each other. Since there are so many ways to score, there are hundreds of different styles of scorecard printed. As long as you can follow what is going on in the game, and you are having fun, that's all that really matters.

Other Scoring Symbols

More things happen in baseball games than just hits and outs. Here is a more thorough list of the common scoring symbols. To use these, just write the symbol in the box of the player who was out or advanced a base.

BB	Base on balls; or, you can write W for walk
K	Strikeout. If the batter struck out looking (meaning he just stood there while the umpire called a pitch over home plate for strike three) then you can write a backwards K.
HBP	Hit by pitch
SF	Sacrifice fly
S or SAC	Sacrifice bunt
E#	Error, followed by the number of the fielder that made the error. For example, an error by the second baseman would be written E4.
DP	Double play (including the fielder numbers involved in the play)
TP	Triple play (including the fielder numbers involved in the play). Triple plays are extremely rare, so if you score one of these, save the scorecard.

G   Ground ball. If it's not clear that the ball was hit on the ground, write a G.

L   Line drive

F   Usually means that the ball was in foul territory when it was caught. A foul pop up to the catcher would be scored 2F.

This game goes on, and on, and on...

Extra Innings

Use the clue under the blank space to come up with a word. Write this word in the box. When you add the word "IN", the new word has a totally different meaning!

1. _____ I N = to start
   (to plead for money)

2. _____ I N = small house in the woods
   (taxi)

3. _____ I N = springtime bird with red breast
   (steal)

4. _____ I N = heavy, shiny fabric
   (past tense of SIT)

5. _____ I N = penguin-like bird with colorful beak
   (short breath out)

Other symbols you might use that don't describe what the batter did, but often tell you that the runners moved up, can be put in a corner of the box:

SB   Stolen base.

CS   Caught stealing (include the fielder numbers involved in the play)

PB   Passed ball—this is when the catcher drops a ball he should have caught, allowing a runner to advance

WP   Wild pitch—this is when a pitch is so bad that the catcher didn't have a good chance to catch it, and a runner advances.

Baseball Scoring Questions and Answers

When a team wins a game, how do you know who the winning pitcher is when more than one pitcher played for the team?

How Do You Decide Who Is the Winning Pitcher?

Every game has a winning and losing pitcher. The winning pitcher is the one who was pitching for the winning team at the time they took the lead and did not lose the lead again.

For example, if Josh Beckett starts a game for the Red Sox against the Indians and the Red Sox take a 4–0 lead in the early innings and go on to win the game 4–3, Beckett will be the winning pitcher since they never gave up the lead.

However, if the Indians come back and tie the game and the Red Sox bring in a relief pitcher in the seventh inning and then score two runs in the eighth and win 6–4, the

Keeping Score

relief pitcher would get the win because he was the pitcher when his team took the lead and didn't lose it again.

Starting pitchers get more wins because they pitch more innings. A starting pitcher must go five innings to earn a win, but a reliever can earn the win no matter how few batters he faces.

Losing pitchers are determined in the opposite way. If a pitcher gives up the runs that put the other team ahead and his team never catches up, then he gets the loss.

What Does the Official Scorer Do?

The official scorer is someone at every game (often a sports journalist) whose job is to decide how to score certain plays. The scorer will decide if a ball that a fielder drops or throws badly is a hit or an error. Official scorers also decide whether a pitch is a wild pitch or a passed ball, and they make other, more obscure, scoring decisions. Official scorers

The Difference Between Radio and Television

Phil Rizzuto, the Hall of Fame Yankee shortstop of the 1950s, became a commentator with the Yankees after he retired. Rizzuto once said: "I like radio better than television because if you make a mistake on radio, they don't know. You can make up anything on the radio."

decide only how the game is recorded statistically—they cannot overrule an umpire's call.

When Was the First Scorecard Used?

The first scorecard was created by the Knickerbocker ball club way back in 1845.

Why do the Managers and Umpires Meet at Home Plate Before Every Game?

You may notice that before each game there is a short meeting between the umpires and the managers or coaches. This meeting has two purposes. The first is to exchange the lineup cards—each manager hands the umpire and the opposing manager a copy of his lineup. After the meeting, no more changes are allowed to the lineup.

The second purpose is to discuss the ground rules. Every stadium is built differently, and it's important that everyone understands the specific rules for what is considered in-play and what is foul territory. Some ballparks have a line on a high fence. If the ball is over that line it's a home run. Other stadiums have a high wall, but the rule is if it hits the wall, it's not a home run but still in play. Everything about the field needs to be talked about so there are no problems with the rules during the game. You probably do the same thing before playing any game with your friends, when you stop and go over the rules.

A Portion of a Sample Scorecard

In the previous chapter you learned how to read the box score from the October 2, 2004, game between the Dodgers and the Giants. Here's the Dodgers' half of a scorecard from that game.

The Magic Number

Near the end of the baseball season teams start to figure out the "magic number." This is how many games the leading team must win, and how many games any other team must lose, for the leader to win the pennant (championship in their league).

There's some tricky math here. Pretend you have two teams—Team A and Team X. Team A is the leading team in the league, having won the most games so far. Team X is any other team in the league.

Follow the steps below using the scores from our sample teams. You can use the same steps with your favorite teams!

The season has 162 scheduled games.

	won	lost	
TEAM A	93	59	games played so far: 152
TEAM X	89	63	

Games TEAM X has won _____

ADD games TEAM X has left _____

SUBTRACT games TEAM A has won _____

ADD the number 1 _____

THE MAGIC NUMBER

135

Most of this game was pretty easy to score. For example, look at the fourth inning: Finley flied out to right field, Beltre flied out to center field, and Green flied out to center field. In fact, one of the things this scorecard can tell you that the box score can't is that the Dodgers hit a *lot* of fly balls, but that most of them were caught.

When a pinch hitter comes to the plate, you draw a heavy line before the box when he comes up. Look at Mayne's spot in the seventh inning. The heavy line means that Mayne was replaced with pinch hitter Grabowski; but the K means that Grabowski struck out.

When a new pitcher comes into the game, you draw a heavy line before the first batter he faces. For example, in the eighth inning, a new pitcher came in to face Finley, and *another* new pitcher came in to face Beltre.

The ninth inning of this scorecard is kind of complicated. Go through it batter by batter to find out what happened. Green led off the inning with a single, and then Ventura walked. Cora struck out looking. Hernandez pinch-hit, and he walked to load the bases. Choi pinch-hit, and he also walked, forcing in a run. A new pitcher came in. Izturis reached first base on an error by the shortstop, scoring Ventura. A new pitcher came in. Werth singled, scoring a third run. Another new pitcher came in. (That's a *lot* of pitchers for one inning.) Then Finley hit a home run to win the game—the GS stands for grand slam. Since this inning had so much going on and was so exciting, you might choose to make a few notes about it at the bottom of the scorecard page. Now, if you're a Dodger fan, you might ask Steve Finley to autograph this scorecard, frame it, and put it on the wall of your room. Of course, if you're a Giants fan, you might just put the scorecard in your desk drawer and try to forget about it.

Sample Scorecard

This is how a scorecard is done.

DATE: October 2, 2004
Los Angeles Dodgers (vs. San Francisco Giants) at Dodger Stadium

FINAL SCORE: SF 3

Pos.	Name	1	2	3	4	5	6	7	8	9	10	11
SS	Izturis	G3		8		2F			8	◆ E6	RBI	
LF	Werth	K		8			3		1B	◆ 1B	RBI	
CF	Finley	1B			9		4L		4-3	◆ HR	^{4}RBI	
3B	Beltre	8	1B		8		5-3	9	6-3	GS		
RF	Green				8	3-1		9		◆ 1B		
1B	Ventura		K			W E8		K		◆ W		
2B	Cora		5					W		K		
C	Mayne/ PH Grabowski (7th), PH J. Hernandez (9th)		9					K		◆ W	RBI	
P	Dessens/ PH Saenz (8th), PH Choi (9th)			7		5-3			1B	◆ W	RBI	

What kind of baseball players practice in the Arctic Circle?

Color in each box with a dot in the upper right-hand corner to find the silly answer to this riddle:

Chapter 10
Beyond the Game

commons: Commons are cards of average players, not superstars. These cards aren't usually valuable to professional collectors, but they still might have value to you or to a friend if the player is one of your favorites or if that player is on your favorite team.

Baseball fans love to go to games, watch games, read about games, and tell stories about games. But there are even more ways to enjoy baseball! This chapter describes two popular baseball-related activities: collecting baseball cards, and playing fantasy baseball. Even if you've never tried either before, you might find that these are great ways to gain more knowledge of baseball, meet and hang out with fellow fans, and enjoy a new hobby.

Baseball Cards

Baseball cards are playing-card size, with a picture of a player on one side and his career stats with a short description of his career highlights on the other side. Your card collection is a reflection of your favorite teams and your favorite players, but as you get older, your collection can help store memories of seasons gone by.

Acquiring Baseball Cards

Baseball cards can be bought at many different kinds of stores. Grocery or convenience stores will often have packs of cards. Department stores or discount outlets might have a wider selection. Specialist card stores and dealers will have rare or especially interesting cards.

Cards come in packs of seven, ten, twelve, or more, depending on the company and the type of pack you buy. Many companies make baseball cards, each with a different look. Topps, Donruss, and Upper Deck are among the most popular card-making companies. Most packs include a random assortment of current players—the fun is seeing which players you get when you open the pack. New cards come out every season, as they have since the early 1900s.

Most card buyers enjoy collecting the cards for the fun of it. The cards themselves have a glossy look and the photos are sometimes really cool action shots from the game. The statistics on the back of the cards give you all sorts of information about how the player has done in his career. Reading your cards can teach you a lot about your favorite players, so that the next time you see them in a game, you have a better appreciation for who they are and where they've come from.

There are more serious collectors who buy and sell older or special cards for lots of money. Card shows, online card dealers, and auctions are places where adults who are in the baseball card business can buy and sell valuable cards. But baseball card collecting is *not* about monetary value—it's about savoring the game of baseball.

Dugout

One letter has been dug out of each of the following common baseball words. Fill in the missing letters. Then, transfer those letters to the corresponding boxes in the grid to form the answer to this riddle:

What's another nickname for a baseball bat?

1. U N I _ O R M
2. G _ O V E
3. P L A _ O F F
4. _ L I D E
5. S _ I N G
6. F _ N
7. B U N _
8. C A _ C H E R
9. S T _ A L
10. _ U N

1	2	3	4	5	6	7	8	9	10

Collectible Cards

Sometimes the most valuable cards are those that accidentally get printed with a few mistakes or differences. Can you find the nine differences between these two cards?

Collectible Words

See if you can collect nine words hiding in the word **COLLECTIBLE**.

Extra Fun: Try to have all nine words use only four letters.

Some Baseball Card History

Professional baseball began at the end of the 1860s, and by the late 1880s the first baseball cards were printed. These early cards were printed on the cardboard backs of cigarette packs. Top players of the day like Cap Anson and Buck Ewing were among the first players to appear on cards. Pretty soon, in the early 1900s, a number of cigarette manufacturers were printing cards of the best players, such as Ty Cobb and Honus Wagner. There were far fewer copies of each card printed than there are of cards today.

By the 1930s chewing gum companies were also making baseball cards, and collecting these cards was becoming more popular. In 1933 the Goudey Chewing Gum Company accidentally forgot to print card number 106 in their set, a card of all-star (and future Hall-of-Famer) Napoleon LaJoie. So many collectors sent letters asking for the missing card that the company had to print more in 1934, and it sent them to the people who had written in. This was one of the first indications that card collecting was becoming popular.

Then, in 1952, Topps made its first baseball cards with statistics of the players on the back. Through the 1960s and '70s card collecting was very popular, but it wasn't until the late 1980s that rich collectors began to pay high prices for old cards, and baseball cards were seen by some as an investment, like putting money in the stock market. Today, card collecting isn't quite as popular as it was at the start of the 1990s, but it is still done by many, many fans.

Why Do Some Cards Cost More Than Others?

For one thing, the greater players are more expensive because everyone knows them. Older cards, like those from the 1940s, '50s, or '60s usually cost more than cards from the '70s or '80s because they are harder to find. Not many

FUN FACT

The Most Expensive Card Ever

Pirates shortstop Honus Wagner did not want his card associated with cigarettes, so he asked that the tobacco company stop printing his cards. Therefore, only a few cards of this legendary player exist. His 1909 card, known to collectors as T-206, is now so rare that at an auction in New York City it sold for $640,000.

Stick of Gum

Once upon a time, one of the things you would always find in a pack of baseball cards was a long, pink stick of chewing gum. This isn't very common anymore, but it was standard for many years.

people saved them, so they are more expensive since there aren't too many around. When a lot of people want something, like a rare card, the person who owns it can ask for more money since people can't go out and find that card elsewhere. Cards that have a "defect," or a mistake, on them are also expensive since they are very rare, and usually the mistake was corrected by the company after they printed the first few. Sometimes a word is off-center or even spelled wrong. A couple of times a company printed the wrong name on the wrong picture. Now that's a big mistake—and an expensive card.

Sometimes the cost might depend on where you are buying a card. For example, in St. Louis an Albert Pujols rookie card would sell for more than in New York because he is a Cardinals fan favorite. In New York, however, a Derek Jeter card would be more expensive than in St. Louis because he is a Yankee.

What Should You Do with Your Baseball Cards?

The easy answer to that question is—anything you want, especially anything that makes collecting cards fun. Here are some ideas of ways to enjoy your collection.

- **Read your cards:** You may *think* you know everything about your favorite player, but you might be surprised by some new information on that player's card. You also might learn something about a player that makes you like him more—for example, he may have grown up in your hometown, or he may have gone to your favorite college.
- **Trade with your friends:** If you are buying lots of packs of cards, you will end up with several copies of the same player's card. Offer to give a duplicate to a friend if your friend will give you a card that you

really want. Or, say you're trying to collect the whole starting lineup for your favorite team. You might be able to fill in the cards you don't have by trading.

- **Use cards as decorations:** Is the wall behind your desk or over your bed bare? Does your locker need something on the door? Use baseball cards to decorate. You could change the players in your decoration every month or every year based on how the players do.

- **Collect groups of players that are special:** Of course, you want to collect cards of your favorite players. But you might also try to get the whole roster of your town's home team. Or this year's all-star team. Or the ten pitchers with the most victories. Or the batters who lead the league in home runs, RBIs, and batting average. Or last year's MVPs and Cy Young Award winners. Pick any category of players that interests you, and go get their cards!

- **Make albums:** You can organize your cards in photo albums, or even in albums specially designed for baseball cards. Albums allow you to look at many sets of cards at once; they also keep the cards in good condition in a place where you won't lose them.

- **Get autographs:** If you know that you might have a chance to get a player's autograph—say, you have front-row tickets to a game, or you're going to hear a player speak—bring that player's card, and you can ask the player to sign the card.

- **Anything else you can think of!** Some people think of their cards as a financial investment. They collect cards only because they think the cards will be worth lots of money someday. Well, it's *extremely* unlikely that your card collection will be ever be worth much more than you paid for it. So if you want to put baseball cards in the spokes of your bicycle, or if you

WHIP: WHIP stands for "Walks plus Hits per Inning Pitched." Many leagues keep track of this category, which means almost the same thing as base runners per inning. Only the very best pitchers' WHIP is below 1.000. A good WHIP is 1.100 or 1.150.

keepers: Once you've played fantasy baseball with the same people for a few years, you might make a rule that owners can choose some players from this year's team to be on their team again next year. A player who stays with the same team two years in a row is called a "keeper."

cheat sheets: Rankings of the best players are called "cheat sheets." Don't start a draft without one! You can make cheat sheets yourself; or, you can find many magazines and Web sites with their own cheat sheets that you can use.

want to play games with them outside, or if you want to nail them to your wall, do it! The whole point of card collecting is to have fun. Anything you can do with your cards that you think is fun is worth doing.

Fantasy Baseball

Have you ever wanted to own a baseball team? If so, you should start saving your money now—it costs close to a billion dollars to buy a major-league team. But you and your friends can run your own fantasy baseball teams this season without paying any money at all.

In fantasy baseball, you choose major-league players to be on your team. The better your players perform, the better your team does. Since you're in charge of your team, you can make trades, bench players who aren't doing well, set starting lineups, put players on the disabled list . . . you can do pretty much everything a real baseball owner does.

How Fantasy Baseball Works

Fantasy baseball teams are ranked based on statistics. Usually a league keeps track of 10 categories (see the sidebar). Your team gets credit for the statistics of all players in your starting lineup. If one of your players hits a home run, your team gets a home run. If one of your pitchers strikes out eight batters, your team adds eight strikeouts to its total.

In *head-to-head* leagues, each week you play a "game" against another team in your league. You have to do better than your opponent in each category. For example, if your pitchers record five saves this week, but your opponent's pitchers only record four saves, then you win the "saves" category. If you win more categories than your opponent, then you win the game! Whichever team wins the most games by the end of the year is the champion.

In *rotisserie* leagues, you add up your statistics for the whole season. In each category you get points for every team you beat. Whoever gets the most points at the end of the season is the league champion.

Determining Who's on Your Team

All fantasy baseball owners want Albert Pujols on their team. But he can only be on one team in each league. So how do you decide who gets which players? There are two common methods: the *draft* and the *auction*. The draft is simpler and is recommended for new players. Advanced players can try out an auction.

In a fantasy baseball draft, teams take turns selecting players. On your turn, you can choose any player who hasn't already been chosen. But you have to be sure to fill every position on your team!

In an auction, each team is given a budget of pretend money, say, $100. A player is mentioned, then each team can bid for that player. Whoever bids the most money gets the player. But you only have that $100 for your whole team. Spend too much on one player, and you'll be stuck without money to fill out your roster.

After the draft or auction, you still have to manage your team. If one of your players gets hurt, or isn't doing well, you'll need to replace him. The easiest way to obtain players is through "waivers." Players who aren't on a team are listed on the "waiver wire." You can choose a player from this list to be on your team. Each league makes rules about how often you can pick up one of these players, and about what happens if two teams want the same player.

FUN FACT

Scoring a Rotisserie League

Let's say you are playing in a six-team league. The best team in each category would earn six points; the second-best team, five points; and so on. Consider the "batting average" category:

Batting Averages

Team Name	average	points
Electric Marshmallows	.310	6
Varied Buntings	.303	5
Water Foul	302	4
Bay Area Bombers	.296	3
Area 51 Greenmen	.280	2
Frumious Bandersnachi	.278	1

The nine other categories are scored the same way. Then, you add up each team's total points in all categories to see who wins.

Public Leagues

If you can't find enough friends to make a fantasy league, try joining a "public league" on a fantasy baseball Web site. You will be matched with other players of similar experience.

Another option for improving your team is to make trades. If your team has plenty of one statistic but needs to do better in another, you might consider a trade. For example, your team might have a whole lot of saves, but not very many stolen bases. So, you could offer to give another team one of your closers, like Mariano Rivera, in exchange for someone who steals a lot of bases, like Jose Reyes.

Fantasy Baseball Strategy

The fantasy team owners who do the best are the ones who pay careful attention to the players. Sure, you want to pick players who are stars, and players whom everyone knows about. But pretty soon after your draft starts, there won't be any stars left. So how do you know which players to pick?

Before your draft, you should read about every team. Find out what new players are on the team. Know who is likely to start at each position. Then, make a list of who you think are the best 10 or 15 major-league players at each position, and a list of the 30 or so players you absolutely want if you can have them.

After the draft, it's usually a good idea to leave your team alone for a few weeks to see how your players do. Be careful—in the excitement of the early season, it's tempting to give up on a good player who starts with a slump; it's tempting to pick up a poorer player who happens to be off to a hot start. More often than not, though, you'll do best by sticking with your players who have a history of producing strong stats. The only major exception is if one of your players is injured, or if he starts losing playing time—then it might be time to make a move.

Who Keeps Track of Your League?

Years ago, people who played fantasy baseball had to keep careful track of their team by reading newspaper box scores every day and writing down each player's stats. Nowadays, though, the Internet makes keeping track of your team's stats simple. Some Internet fantasy baseball services are free, like those at yahoo.com or sportsline.com. For your first season of fantasy baseball, a free service will work fine—your parents can easily help you sign up with one of these.

There are other Web sites that require a registration fee to play. These sites will usually provide more options for which stats your league can use, and will usually provide more detailed and even live scoring updates, along with message boards and "expert" advice. But you don't need to pay to play fantasy baseball unless you're an advanced enough player to really want these extra features.

The neatest thing about fantasy baseball is how much you learn about major-league players. Fantasy leagues also give you baseball topics to talk to your friends about. Try owning a team for a season—you'll probably appreciate the *real* game of baseball even more due to your fantasy experience.

FUN FACT

Which Stats Does Your League Use?

The most common leagues keep track of 10 statistics. For offensive players, your team earns points for batting average, home runs, runs batted in, stolen bases, and runs. Pitchers earn points for wins, saves, strikeouts, earned run average, and base runners per inning. But you can find (or create) a league that keeps track of pretty much any stats.

Name Game

This baseball card collector has gotten some pretty famous autographs. Unfortunately, the players signed their names too big! Can you tell who signed each card? Choose names from the list.

Barry Bonds
Willie Mays
Nolon Ryan
Pete Rose
Alex Rodriguez
Cy Young
Sandy Koufax
Ty Cobb
Jimmie Foxx
Tom Seaver
Greg Maddux
Lou Gehrig
Hank Aaron

Glossary

assist

When a player makes a throw of any kind to get an out, whether it's an infielder throwing a batter out running to first base or an outfielder throwing a runner out at home plate, the player gets an assist.

backstop

The fence behind home plate is the backstop. In parks and on little league fields, the backstop is usually a high fence that slants over home plate so that foul balls don't fly off and hurt people passing by. (Backstop is also a slang term used for a catcher.)

battery

Battery is a term for the pitcher and catcher. If, for example, Mike Hampton is pitching and Mike Piazza is catching, they are "the battery" in that game.

batting order

The order in which players on a team come up and take their turn as the hitter. The manager or coach of the team decides the batting order before the game and lists the players, first through ninth, in order of when they will hit. If a batter bats out of turn he is called out.

bleachers

The seats behind the outfield wall are called the bleachers. Sometimes, like in Wrigley Field, the fans who sit there call themselves the "bleacher bums."

blooper

A blooper is a ball that is not hit very hard but sort of pops over the infielders and lands in front of the outfielders for a hit.

box score

A box score is a grid containing a summary of the game statistics, including how each player did.

bullpen

The bullpen is where the relief pitchers warm up before coming in to pitch. Most stadiums have bullpens beyond the outfield fences, while some have them in foul territory.

bunt

To bunt is to hold the bat horizontally, one hand on the handle and the other way up on the bat (don't hold it with your hand around the front of the bat, just pinch it from the back part so your finger doesn't get squished by the pitch). The idea is to let the ball just bounce off the bat and stay fair so the runners can move up a base, which is known as a "sacrifice." You can also bunt for a hit by pushing the bat so that the ball rolls a little farther toward third base or first base.

cleanup hitter

The cleanup hitter is the fourth hitter in the lineup.

closer

The relief pitcher that comes in to get the final outs

and the save is the team's "closer."

commentators

The commentators are the broadcasters or announcers who are at the ballpark describing what is going on in the game on either television or radio.

commons

Commons are cards of average players, not superstars. These cards aren't usually valuable to professional collectors; but they still might have value to you or to a friend if the player is one of your favorites, or if that player is on your favorite team.

contact hitter

A contact hitter is one that makes contact with the ball often and doesn't strike out very much.

count

The count is the number of balls and strikes that have been pitched to the hitter. For example, two balls and two strikes would be a "two and two" count.

dinger

Dinger is a slang term for a home run.

disabled list

When a player is injured the team may put the player on what is called "the disabled list," or dl. This means the player cannot play for fifteen or more days and the team can call someone else up from the minor leagues to put on their roster of active players.

double

You get safely to second base.

double play

A double play is when two players get called out after one player hits the ball.

error

When a fielder drops or bobbles a ball or throws it so the other fielder can't catch it and it results in the batter or runner being safe, it's called an error on the fielder.

extra innings

If a game is tied after the regulation nine innings, teams go into extra innings, which means they play additional innings until someone scores the winning run or runs. The home team always gets the last turn at bat.

fan

Besides being one of the people rooting for your favorite team, to "fan" in baseball is another term for striking out.

foul ball

A ball that is hit that is not in fair territory. Foul balls count as strike one and strike two, but not as strike three unless you're bunting. In the big leagues, many foul balls go into the stands and are souvenirs to the fans who catch them.

foul line

The lines extending from home plate past first and third base all the way to the outfield fence that separate fair territory from foul territory.

foul out

When a ball is hit in the air in foul territory and caught by an opposing player for an out.

foul pole

A ball that flies over the outfield fence is only a home run if it leaves the field in fair territory. The foul poles make it easy to tell whether a ball is a home run: One side of the pole is fair, the other is foul. But if the ball hits the foul pole, it's a home run.

foul territory

The part of the playing field that is outside of the foul lines and not part of the actual field of play.

full count

Three balls and two strikes is considered a full count—one more ball is a walk and one more strike is a strikeout.

grand slam

A grand slam is when you hit a home run with the bases loaded (a player on each base). The most runs you can score on one hit are on a grand slam!

head-to-head

A type of fantasy league in which your team's stats are compared to one other team's stats on a week-by-week basis.

hit and run

A "hit and run" play is where the base runners start running and the batter is supposed to hit the ball on the ground or for a base hit. This play helps avoid a double play and can also get runners to advance more bases on a base hit.

hits

A player gets a hit when he or she hits the ball and then runs to the base without making an out. Here are the different kinds of hits you can get: single, double, triple, and home run.

home run

You touch all the bases including home plate (where you start from as the batter). If you hit one over the fence, it's a home run and you should be very happy!

home team

The team most of the local fans root for since they are the team hosting the game on their field. The home team always bats second in the inning, or in the "bottom of the inning."

inning

An inning is a period of play in which each team has a turn at bat. Each team gets three outs. A regulation baseball game lasts nine innings.

inside-the-park home run

Most home runs go over the outfield fence, but a fast runner might be able to get all the way around the bases on a ball that stays in the ballpark on an inside-the-park homer— it's very rare!

intentional walk

An intentional walk, sometimes called an intentional pass, is when a pitcher walks a batter on purpose. Sometimes this makes it easier to get a double play if there are other runners on second and/or third. Sometimes a batter is walked intentionally because the player is very good and the pitcher doesn't want to give up a home run.

left on base

You may see this in the box score (lob) or hear broadcasters mention it. This indicates how many players were left standing on the bases when the final out was made to end an inning.

mound

The mound, or pitching mound, is the dirt circle in the middle of the infield diamond where the pitcher stands.

on deck

The batter who is scheduled to hit next is considered to be waiting "on deck." Usually there is an on-deck circle where the player stands and takes practice swings.

opposite field

When the announcer says a hitter got a hit to the opposite field, it means the ball went the opposite way from where it should go for that type of hitter. When the bat is swung around, most left-handed hitters will hit the ball to right field, and right-handed hitters will hit the ball to left field. If the hitter hits it to the other field, a right-handed hitter hitting to right field and vice versa, it's called hitting to the opposite field.

overrun

This is when you are going too fast and run over the base. You're allowed to overrun first base, but if you overrun second or third, you can be tagged out.

pennant

The team that wins the National League or American League Championship is said to have won the pennant—then they play in the World Series.

pickoff

If there's a base runner and the pitcher throws to the fielder, who catches the runner off base and tags that runner for an out, it's called a pickoff.

pinch hitter

A pinch hitter is a hitter who bats in place of someone else.

pinch runner

A pinch runner is a player who comes in to run for someone else. This may be a faster runner who can steal a base or score a run more easily.

prospect

A player who is thought to have skills that will make that player a future star is considered to be a prospect.

putout

Whenever a fielder catches a ball that results in an out, it's a putout. This includes a first baseman taking a throw from an infielder and stepping on the base, or a catcher on a strikeout.

rain delay

A rain delay is when the game is stopped because of rain, but they hope to continue and finish it later. The umpires decide when to stop, restart, or call a game (cancel it) because of rain.

rain out

A rain out is when a game is called off because of rain. If this happens before the fifth inning, the game doesn't count. If it's after the fifth inning it's considered an official game, and whichever team was ahead at the time wins.

reliever

A reliever or relief pitcher is the pitcher who comes in to replace the starting pitcher.

rookie

A first-year player is also known as a rookie.

roster

A roster is the listing of players on the team. Major-league rosters include 25 players for most of the season.

rotisserie

A type of fantasy baseball league in which your team's stats are compared to other team's stats for the whole year.

run

A "run" in baseball is scored whenever a player comes all the way around the bases and crosses home plate. The team who scores the most runs wins.

rundown play

When a runner is trapped between bases, the fielders play what looks like a game of monkey-in-the-middle as they throw the ball back and forth trying to tag the runner and not let him or her get to the next base. Usually a runner will be called out in a rundown play unless one of the fielders misses the ball.

save

When a pitcher comes into a close ballgame and gets the final outs it is called a save.

scoring position

When a runner is on second or third base, he is considered in scoring position, meaning it's easier to score on a hit.

signs

Some people hold up signs in the stands, but in baseball there are other signs. The catcher puts down fingers to give the pitcher a sign as to what pitch to throw. There are also signs relayed from the coach at third base to the batter. Coaches are usually busy touching their cap,

tugging on their ear, and doing all sorts of movements. They are signaling the batter to take a pitch, swing away, bunt, or perhaps hit and run. They are also often signaling runners on base. Next time you're at a game, watch the third base coach for a minute and see what he's up to. If you're playing, always check what the sign from the coach is before the pitcher pitches.

single

You get to first base safely without anyone catching the ball in the air, tagging you out, or throwing to first base before you get there.

slide

A slide is when a runner dives feet first or head first into a base. Be careful if you try sliding—ask your coach to help you learn how to slide properly so you don't get hurt.

southpaw

A left-handed pitcher is sometimes referred to as a southpaw.

spitball or "spitter"

Once upon a time, in the early years of baseball, it used to be okay for pitchers to spit on the ball before throwing it. It made the ball make some strange movements, and batters had a hard time hitting it. The rules no longer allow this pitch to be thrown.

starter

The starter is the pitcher that begins pitching the game for the team.

take

To "take" a pitch means to not swing at it. If a pitcher is having trouble throwing strikes, a batter may take a pitch to see if the pitcher can throw it in the strike zone. If the batter has three balls and no strikes, she will almost always take the pitch to try and get a walk.

tarp

The tarp is what the grounds crew covers the field with while the teams, umpires, and fans wait for the rain to stop so they can continue the game. The tarp is a giant piece of plastic that usually just covers the infield.

triple

You get safely to third base.

triple play

A triple play is a very rare play where one player hits the ball and all three outs are made. Naturally, there has to be no one out and at least two runners on base for a triple play.

umpire

An umpire is the person who is refereeing the game or ruling on the plays in the game. The umpire rules whether a pitch is a strike or a ball, if a ball that is hit is fair or foul, or if a batter or runner is safe or out.

visiting team

The team that comes to play on another team's field. The visiting team always bats first in the inning, known as the "top of the inning."

walk-off home run

This refers to a home run in the bottom of the ninth or in the home team's at bat in the bottom of an extra inning that wins and ends the game. Following the home run, the teams walk off the field—hence the name.

WHIP

Walks plus Hits per Inning Pitched is an important statistical category for fantasy baseball. Anything below 1.2 is pretty good.

wild card

In major-league baseball there are three divisions in each league, but four teams make the playoffs each year. The fourth team, the wild card team, is the best second-place team from any one of the three divisions.

Appendix B
Extra Innings: **Books, Magazines, Web Sites, and More**

Baseball Books

Historical Baseball Books

The Sporting News Selects: Baseball's 25 Greatest Moments by Ron Smith and Joe Morgan.

The All-Century Team by Mark Vancil looks at the 100 best players of the 20th century.

The Story of The Negro Leagues by William Brashler has the history and the stars of these leagues.

300 Great Baseball Cards of the 20th Century is a historical look at baseball cards from Beckett Publishing.

The Echoing Green: The Untold Story of Bobby Thomson, Ralph Branca, and the Shot Heard Round the World by Joshua Prager gives details about how the Giants were stealing catchers' signs from their center field clubhouse, leading to Thomson's famous home run.

How to Play the Game

Jeff Burroughs' Little League Instructional Guide

Baseball for Kids: Skills, Strategies and Stories to Make You a Better Ballplayer by Jerry Kasoff

Touching All the Bases: Baseball for Kids of All Ages by Claire MacKay

The Art of Pitching by Tom Seaver

The Art of Hitting by Tony Gwynn

The Science of Hitting by Ted Williams

Biographies

Jackie and Me (about Jackie Robinson), *Babe and Me*, and *Honus and Me* (about Honus Wagner) are in the Baseball Card Adventure series by Dan Gutman.

Lou Gehrig, Pride of the Yankees by Keith Brandt

Babe Ruth, Home Run Hero by Keith Brandt

I Had a Hammer: The Hank Aaron Story by Lonnie Wheeler with Hank Aaron himself

Lists, Quotes, Jokes, and Statistics

Yogisms: I Didn't Really Say Everything I Said by Yogi Berra has a lot of the funniest sayings by one funny former catcher.

Total Baseball: The Official Encyclopedia of Major League Baseball by John Thorn is loaded with statistics and very heavy.

Baseball Prospectus: The Essential Guide to the Baseball Season is a yearly guide that includes comprehensive statistics and analysis. It's a great tool to help prepare for a fantasy baseball season.

Batter Up! Baseball Activities for Kids of All Ages by Ouisie Shapiro.

You can even work on your math skills and have some fun with:

Baseball Math: Grandslam Activities and Projects for Grades 4–8 by Christopher Jennison.

Baseball Movies

The Pride of the Yankees, 1942. This is the story of Lou Gehrig.

The Babe Ruth Story, 1948.

The Jackie Robinson Story, 1950.

Angels in the Outfield, 1951, the original. This film was remade in 1994.

Damn Yankees, 1958.

Bang the Drum Slowly, 1973.

The Bad News Bears, 1976.

The Natural, 1984.

Eight Men Out, 1988, about the 1919 Black Sox scandal.

Field of Dreams, 1989.

Major League, 1989.

A League of Their Own, 1992, about the women's leagues of the 1940s.

Magazines

Baseball Digest

This is a monthly magazine with stories about pro players past and present, rosters, a quiz (it's not easy), a crossword puzzle, and plenty of fun facts about the game.

Baseball Weekly

Baseball Weekly is a magazine devoted to the latest info on the major leagues and even the minor leagues. Plenty of statistics and recent box scores are included in *Baseball Weekly*.

Junior League Baseball

Junior League Baseball is all about baseball leagues for players 7 to 17.

Sporting News

The *Sporting News* is the weekly newspaper of all sports. During the spring and summer months, there are plenty of stories about baseball plus lots of neat stats.

Sports Illustrated for Kids

Sports Illustrated for Kids has info on many sports, including baseball. The magazine includes stuff about playing the game and about your favorite players.

USA Today

USA Today has a great sports section with a lot about baseball, including daily reports on each team so you can see what your favorite team is up to.

Web Sites

MLB.com

This is the major leagues' official baseball Web site. You can find anything you need there, including up-to-the-inning scores, pitching match-ups for the next several days, injury reports, trades, news, player statistics for every major leaguer, plus info on everything from spring training through the World Series. There is a history section with links to all sorts of baseball records and much, much more. In May and June you can even vote for the players for the All-Star game.
www.mlb.com

Sporting News

This has been one of the leading sports newspapers for many years. If you click on MLB (Major League Baseball) in the upper left on the main page, you'll get the baseball page. You'll find headline news plus a long list on the left-hand side of places you can click on to give you more information, including standings, a scoreboard with up-to-the-inning game info, player bios, team reports, fun and prizes, and much more. The *Sporting News* site covers all the other major sports as well.
www.sportingnews.com

USA Today Sports

This is the home of *USA Today*'s baseball Web site. You can simply type in *www.usatoday.com* and click on baseball in the left-hand column. All the latest scores and info on the day's games are available plus loads of statistics, team schedules, TV schedules, injury reports, pitching match-ups, and team reports.
www.usatoday.com/sports/baseball/front.htm

Negro Leagues Baseball

This is a very informative site about the Negro Leagues. The history, players, and teams are all part of this interesting site. New books are featured, as are several articles that offer insight into an important part of baseball and American history.
www.negroleaguebaseball.com

Puzzle Answers

page 9 • Why do hitters...

Because there are more

to choose from!

page 18 • Stealing Bases

<u>B</u><u>a</u>LTIMOR<u>E</u> ORIOLE<u>S</u>

<u>B</u>OSTON R<u>E</u>D <u>S</u>OX

N<u>E</u>W YORK M<u>E</u>T<u>S</u>

<u>B</u>ROOKLYN DODG<u>E</u>R<u>S</u>

LO<u>S</u> <u>A</u>NGEL<u>E</u>S ANGEL<u>S</u>

<u>A</u>TL<u>A</u>N<u>T</u>A <u>B</u>RAV<u>E</u><u>S</u>

page 11 • Curve Ball

```
F L Y L E B O A R D T O
U P O R R L E R N P O P
G R O M F E S E I R E S
A C U P D A T S C T M D
S S T G I C O S H I R L
T K R U U H H N D S N R
R B O E M O R E P U T O
I O U S R H O T R S G W
H O T T S T O P E S O O
O M D U U H O T M T U B
T D O L R K M M O A T L
R O G D B F E O H D M A
```

page 23 • Hard Ball

page 52 • Play Ball

1.	Print the word BASEBALL.	BASEBALL
2.	Switch the position of the first two letters.	ABSEBALL
3.	Move the 5th letter between the 2nd and 3rd letters.	ABBSEALL
4.	Switch the positions of the 4th and 8th letters.	ABBLEALS
5.	Change the 6th letter to P.	ABBLEPLS
6.	Change the last letter to E.	ABBLEPLE
7.	Change both B's to P's.	APPLEPLE
8.	Change the 7th letter to I.	APPLEPIE

page 62 • Switch Hitter

page 72 • Famous Fungo!

2 A milk pitcher!

3 A catcher's mutt!

1 A pancake batter!

page 63 • Who's Who?

1. The Big Train — 3 Cy Young
2. Tom Terrific — 5 Jimmy Foxx
3. Cyclone — 4 Joe DiMaggio
4. Joltin' Joe — 7 Mickey Mantle
5. Double X — 11 Ozzie Smith
6. Mr. October — 10 Pete Rose
7. The Mick — 12 Randy Johnson
8. Say Hey Kid — 6 Reggie Jackson
9. Stan The Man — 13 Roger Clemens
10. Charlie Hustle — 9 Stan Musial
11. Wizard of Oz — 2 Tom Seaver
12. The Big Unit — 1 Walter Johnson
13. The Rocket — 8 Willie Mays

page 87 • Game Pieces

fly ball

southpaw

home run

bullpen

page 90 • How do you get ...

PLAY BALL!

GAME OVER!

PRACTICE, PRACTICE, PRACTICE!

page 93 • Say What?

Y	O	G	I	,		I		C	A	M	E
H	E	R	E		T	O		H	I	T	,
N	O	T		T	O		R	E	A	D	!

page 97 • Hink Pinks

1. The heavier of two batters.

F A T T E R   B A T T E R

2. Where you throw a bad referee.

U M P   D U M P

3. Nine baseball players shouting at once.

T E A M   S C R E A M

4. The last part of a baseball game when one team has more points.

W I N N I N G   I N N I N G

page 98 • Baseball Diamond

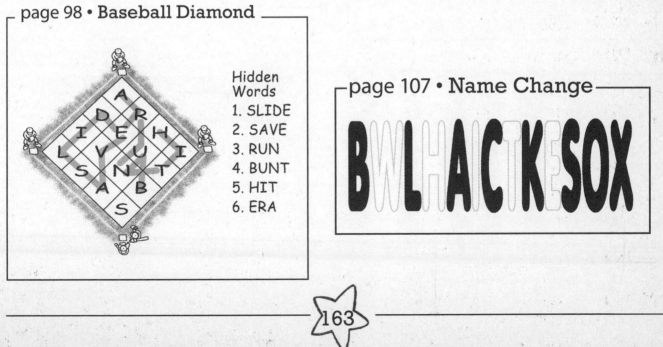

Hidden Words
1. SLIDE
2. SAVE
3. RUN
4. BUNT
5. HIT
6. ERA

page 103 • The "Whole World Series"

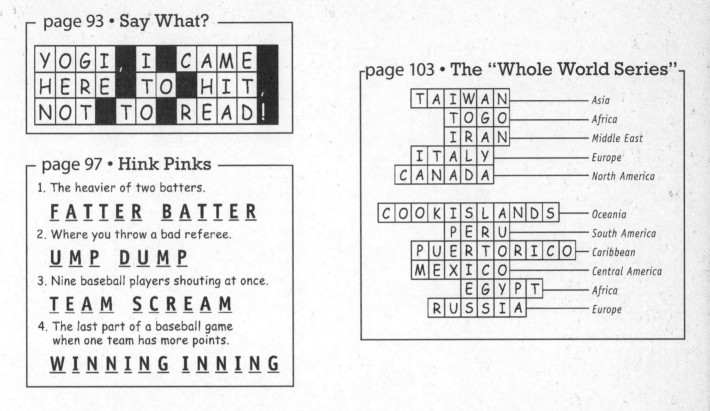

| T | A | I | W | A | N | — Asia
| | T | O | G | O | | — Africa
| | I | R | A | N | | — Middle East
| I | T | A | L | Y | | — Europe
| C | A | N | A | D | A | — North America

| C | O | O | K | I | S | L | A | N | D | S | — Oceania
| | P | E | R | U | | — South America
| P | U | E | R | T | O | R | I | C | O | — Caribbean
| M | E | X | I | C | O | — Central America
| | E | G | Y | P | T | — Africa
| R | U | S | S | I | A | — Europe

page 107 • Name Change

BWLHACITKESOX

page 119 • Lucky Numbers

	9↓	24↓		27↓	13↓
5→	4	1	12→	5	7
11→	5	6	15→	9	6
	17→	3	6	8	
15↓					11↓
16→	7	9	12→	4	8
13→	8	5	4→	1	3

page 122 • Secret Signals

C A R E F U L — T H I S   G U Y

I S   A   P I N C H   H I T T E R !

page 131 • Extra Innings

1. BEG IN = to start
(to plead for money)

2. CAB IN = small house in the woods
(taxi)

3. ROB IN = springtime bird with red breast
(steal)

4. SAT IN = heavy, shiny fabric
(past tense of sit)

5. PUFF IN = penguin-like bird with colorful beak
(short breath out)

page 126 • How come Drew ...

~~AND~~	EVERY	~~CAT~~
TIME	~~GOT~~	HE
~~BAT~~	GETS	~~EAR~~
TO	~~FUR~~	THIRD
~~BUT~~	BASE	~~HIT~~
HE	~~HAT~~	GOES
~~HUT~~	HOME	~~BAG~~

page 135 • The Magic Number

The season has 162 scheduled games.

	won	lost	games played so far: 152
TEAM A	93	59	
TEAM X	89	63	

Games TEAM X has won	89
ADD games TEAM X has left	+ 10
SUBTRACT games TEAM A has won	− 93
ADD the number 1	+ 1
THE MAGIC NUMBER	= 7

page 138 • … Arctic Circle?

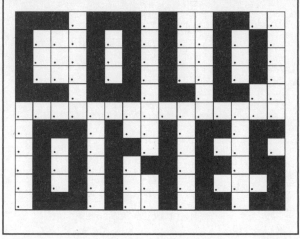

page 142 • Collectible Words

Possible answers to "Collectible Words": toll, bite, cell, bill, tile, belt, coil, bell, tell, till, toil, lilt

page 141 • Dugout

1. UNI**F**ORM
2. G**L**OVE
3. PLA**Y**OFF
4. **S**LIDE
5. SW**I**NG
6. F**A**N
7. BUN**T**
8. CA**T**CHER
9. ST**E**AL
10. **R**UN

1	2	3	4	5	6	7	8	9	10
F	L	Y	S	W	A	T	T	E	R

page 142 • Collectible Cards

page 150 • Name Game

Nolon Ryan — Greg Maddux
Willie Mays — Ty Cobb
Jimmie Foxx — Alex Rodriguez

Index

The Everything® KIDS' Series!

Packed with tons of information, activities, and puzzles, the Everything® Kids' books are perennial bestsellers that keep kids active and engaged.

Each book is $7.95, two-color, 8" x 9¼", and 144 –176 pages.

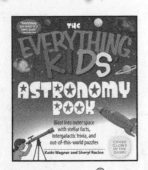

The Everything® Kids'
Astronomy Book
ISBN 10: 1-59869-544-4

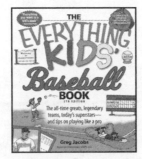

The Everything® Kids' Baseball
Book, 5th Ed.
ISBN 10: 1-59869-487-1

The Everything® Kids' Connect the Dots
Puzzle and Activity Book
ISBN 10: 1-59869-647-5

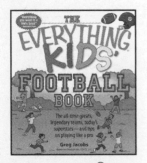

The Everything® Kids'
Football Book
ISBN 10: 1-59869-565-7

The Everything® Kids' Learning
French Book
ISBN 10: 1-59869-543-6

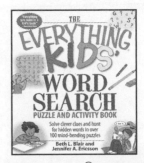

The Everything® Kids' Word
Search Puzzle and Activity Book
ISBN 10: 1-59869-545-2

A silly, goofy, and undeniably icky addition to
the Everything® Kids' series . . .

The Everything® Kids'

GROSS
Series

Chock–full of sickening entertainment for hours of disgusting fun.

The Everything® Kids'
Gross Cookbook
1-59869-324-7, $7.95

The Everything® Kids' Gross
Hidden Pictures Book
1-59337-615-4, $7.95

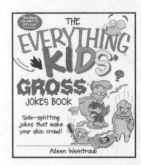

The Everything® Kids'
Gross Jokes Book
1-59337-448-8, $7.95

The Everything® Kids'
Gross Mazes Book
1-59337-616-2, $7.95

The Everything® Kids' Gross
Puzzle & Activity Book
1-59337-447-X, $7.95

Other Everything® Kids' Titles Available

The Everything® Kids' Animal Puzzle & Activity Book
1-59337-305-8

The Everything® Kids' Baseball Book, 4th Ed.
1-59337-614-6

The Everything® Kids' Bible Trivia Book
1-59337-031-8

The Everything® Kids' Bugs Book
1-58062-892-3

The Everything® Kids' Cars and Trucks
Puzzle and Activity Book
1-59337-703-7

The Everything® Kids' Christmas Puzzle
& Activity Book
1-58062-965-2

The Everything® Kids' Cookbook
1-58062-658-0

The Everything® Kids' Crazy Puzzles Book
1-59337-361-9

The Everything® Kids' Dinosaurs Book
1-59337-360-0

The Everything® Kids' Environment Book
1-59869-670-X

The Everything® Kids' Fairies Puzzle and Activity Book
1-59869-394-8

The Everything® Kids' First Spanish Puzzle and
Activity Book
1-59337-717-7

The Everything® Kids' Halloween Puzzle &
Activity Book
1-58062-959-8

The Everything® Kids' Hidden Pictures Book
1-59337-128-4

The Everything® Kids' Horses Book
1-59337-608-1

The Everything® Kids' Joke Book
1-58062-686-6

The Everything® Kids' Knock Knock Book
1-59337-127-6

The Everything® Kids' Learning Spanish Book
1-59337-716-9

The Everything® Kids' Magical Science Experiments Book
1-59869-426-X

The Everything® Kids' Math Puzzles Book
1-58062-773-0

The Everything® Kids' Mazes Book
1-58062-558-4

The Everything® Kids' Money Book
1-58062-685-8

The Everything® Kids' Nature Book
1-58062-684-X

The Everything® Kids' Pirates Puzzle and Activity Book
1-59337-607-3

The Everything® Kids' Presidents Book
1-59869-262-3

The Everything® Kids' Princess Puzzle and Activity Book
1-59337-704-5

The Everything® Kids' Puzzle Book
1-58062-687-4

The Everything® Kids' Racecars Puzzle and Activity Book
1-59869-243-7

The Everything® Kids' Riddles & Brain Teasers Book
1-59337-036-9

The Everything® Kids' Science Experiments Book
1-58062-557-6

The Everything® Kids' Sharks Book
1-59337-304-X

The Everything® Kids' Soccer Book
1-58062-642-4

The Everything® Kids' Spies Puzzle and Activity Book
1-59869-409-X

The Everything® Kids' States Book
1-59869-263-1

The Everything® Kids' Travel Activity Book
1-58062-641-6

All titles are $6.95 or $7.95 unless otherwise noted.

Available wherever books are sold!
To order, call 800-258-0929, or visit us at *www.adamsmedia.com*
Everything® and everything.com® are registered trademarks of F+W Publications, Inc.
Prices subject to change without notice.